Any Saturday, 2021. Running Westward

Newcastle Poetry Prize
Anthology 2021

HUNTER
WRITERS
CENTRE

THE UNIVERSITY OF
NEWCASTLE
AUSTRALIA

Any Saturday, 2021. Running Westward
Newcastle Poetry Prize Anthology 2021

Hunter Writers Centre Inc. and the University of Newcastle
Newcastle NSW 2300

Published by
Hunter Writers Centre inc.
hunterwriterscentre.org

ISBN-978-0-6488504-6-5

Cover design by Laura Kent
Typesetting by HWC Publishing
2021 Published by Hunter Writers Centre Inc.

on a kitchen bench, a sourdough starter silently exhales,
expanding domestic dreams in instagrammable direct-
ions.

~ Lachlan Brown
Any Saturday, 2021. Running Westward
Winner 2021 Newcastle Poetry Prize

Introduction

This year we received poems which covered an enormous amount of ground, thematically and stylistically, from ancient mythology, the incursions of social media into our lives and into poem making, gestures to history and the literary archive, as well as the ageless themes of love, death and the weather. There were a number of poems exploring a return to rural childhoods or a 'bush change'. There were also quite a few ekphrastic poems and journey or road poems, and of course environmental poems, many about fire, and pandemic poems. We were pleased to see more adventurous uses of form and procedure and would have welcomed even more linguistic or formal experimentation, approaches that explore new combinations of form and content that expand a poem's theme, image, feeling and thought in surprising and satisfying ways.

The strength of the Newcastle Poetry Prize is that it encourages both emerging and more established writers to test out new work of an extended nature. However, while the rules of the Prize allow a limit of up to 200 lines, and many poems reached or drew close to that limit, we received a number of strong shorter entries, as shown in some of the runners up and anthology poems.

To bring together an anthology of poems out of the many varied works we read has led us to offer up a type of variousness which is obviously dictated by what was entered into the competition. We are aware that a lot of poets do not enter competitions as a matter of choice or principle, and who do not write what might be termed the 'competition poem'. Nonetheless, we were pleased to find many poems which fully realised the particular styles, themes and procedures that their respective authors had sought to test their poetry ideas with. It goes without saying that there were a number of other poems just outside our reckoning which contained exciting elements, including a fruitful attentiveness to linguistic effects, or intriguing approaches to form or theme which, ultimately, did not quite bring everything together as well as those we finally chose.

1st Prize: Any Saturday, 2021. Running Westward

Any Saturday, 2021. Running Westward emerged early for both of us, and grew in stature with multiple readings, because the poem is multifarious in its treatment of ideation and linguistic play. As its title implies, this poem is a running poem. Taking in the sites/ sights, a kind of inner monologue of the runner navigates through, around and along the edges of a regional centre in western NSW. Its title flows into its first tercet and sets up the continuous leaping from association to association, jogging the reader at each new turn:

> *Any Saturday, 2021. Running Westward*
>
> one-handed pram technique pushing back
> the dawn sky's black activewear. Feeble pieces
> of sleep return or recede like righteous
> seismograph measures. The trees arch over
> this street as though things could be muted
> (the spray of cockatoos shredding leaves /

The poet's sense of humour and touches of irony are distinctive: "the prophecies announce that another / kfc will arise post-covid" and "Isn't nature great?" So too his deliberate mis-spellings of text messages ("kayne west"!) and playful allusion to and inversion of a Robert Frost line. At another level, a sense of the devotional threads through the poem, a metaphysical dimension and appeal to something larger than the suburban and regional setting of the work:

> … think about this rise and fall,
> the moment's monument, the line that corrals reality,
> and shapes the prayers of setting out and return.

Any Saturday is an exemplary long poem and a unanimous winner of the 2021 Newcastle Poetry Prize.

2nd Prize: After 'Still Life with Babette's Jug #2'

After 'Still Life with Babette's Jug #2' is an almost classical ekphrasis in the way it depicts a painting by Anselm van Rood. The more one reads this poem, however, the more surprising it becomes, as each phrase and line opens out its resonances around and beyond the shapes and colours in the painting. Indeed, it lucidly interrogates the concept of colours and allows them to become active presences in the poem. There are also significant edge effects, a ghosting of shadows or suggestive gestures to other shapes and forms—"that centering of white is not where you begin"—as sound also reverberates throughout, mostly via judicious use of alliteration and internal rhyme.

You don't need to have seen the painting to become involved in the way the poem unfolds these ideas and invites the reader into this process, as the poem inventively explores the nature of image making:

> You take a white jug and you see shadows, blues and greys hover
> like halos, like surfaces, like ghosts at the edge of boundaries,
> a thin curving handle like an ear you can see through,
> shapes and triangles of roses and cerulean blue and then black,
> and then the ear becomes an inverted tear, or a cartoon balloon
> for someone to speak, and now the body of the jug's smudges
> take on qualities of the moon while the rim fills with aqua blue
> to swim in …

This poem offers not just a vivid description of a particular image, a painting in this case, but the freshness and richness of lived experience via the dexterous intertwining of image and language effects.

3rd Prize: Ataraxia

Ataraxia is defined as a state of tranquility, free from emotional disturbance and anxiety, and that is exactly what this poem explores and achieves. Sustained through 20 fragments, *Ataraxia* is written with a syntax that is light, sketchy and original. The poem reads like the text equivalent of a diary of hand-drawn pictures, thoughts and events that take place in a sprawling garden or rural property. This is fragment 1:

> in a clearing, just of hours
> the one patch hoped for, blue
>
> we go round with a see-through moon

you go with me in a fold map mulched through
the place is water, spirit pointed in clouds
everything stands up from that

truth dips and perches
years fallow to it

The poem makes wonderful use of wandering, thinking, observation, gardening and subtle philosophising: "you won't tell it's time / for everything as it comes grown in // like blade and fire gone to ground / I live in the land imagined". The writing approaches an imagined asemic state: "let lines run to a tune / glance sideways for the edgewise // having once brushed, join the dots". In a time of such climatic and political upheaval, and social isolation, *Ataraxia* is a balm.

Commended: Poem for My Ancestors

Poem For My Ancestors is a deeply felt meditation on grief, tracing the matriarchal lineage of a Chinese immigrant family. The anecdotes build while the imagery carries the weight of emotion:

… Outside the cemetery gates,

we gathered handfuls of daisies. The sun
burned in the thin sky. Headstones like giant

crusted fingertips thrust from beneath earth.

While the ending is sad it is also uplifting, with the speaker yearning to one day become an ancestor like her forebears.

Commended: Autumn medications

Autumn medications calls on the famous series of eight eight-line poems, 'Autumn Meditations', by Tang Dynasty poet, Du Fu, and has a similar air to that ancient masterpiece's particular observation and melancholy sense of place, as well as memory of old companions, of time wasted. And the list as a device. There is even a brief reference to the Chinese connection in the poem: "That old

Chinese guy down the shops—is that a pipa he's playing?".

But this is the twenty-first century, so instead of meditation we are offered many of the ever-present forms of medication, whether via prescription, over the counter or over the bar, or on the street—"Amoxycillin, Azithromycin, street speed, / nicotine, Hollandia, butterscotch schnapps"—that are both the cause and effect of this poem's precise, at times ironic, and haunted melancholic narrative of medication for pain, however that comes into each life, leading to a cycle of deals and getting through, somehow.

> I missed my chance. I thought I was a little lotus but all
> those little sorrows piled up. So: cover them up, bit by bit.
> Started out on sly pills, nothing much, but oxies
> for the back pain, later. those distant white gulls whirlpooled me.

Harri Jones Memorial Prize: Haruspex

Haruspex is a gnarly poem written "to get to your guts". Its language is spritely, fluid and unusual—unlike anything else submitted to the prize—and updates the conventions of the blazon form, via ancient Rome and the contemporary game Pathologic 2.

We congratulate the winning, commended and shortlisted poets and would like to encourage all who entered, and who keep on with the task of writing poetry. We wish them all ongoing pleasure in their writing and in continuing to offer their best work to readers and audiences, here and elsewhere. We would also like to thank Hunter Writers Centre for facilitating the judging process and the University of Newcastle for the opportunity this prize gives to Australian poets of all kinds. Thank you also to the family of Harri Jones for supporting young poets.

Jill Jones
Toby Fitch

2021 Newcastle Poetry Prize Winners

Winner 2021 Newcastle Poetry Prize
Any Saturday, 2021: Running Westward - Lachlan Brown

2nd Prize
After 'Still Life with Babette's Jug #2' - Gayelene Carbis

3rd Prize
Ataraxia - Christopher (Kit) Kelen

Commended
Autumn Medications - Greg McLaren

Commended
Poem for My Ancestors - Eileen Chong

Harri Jones Memorial Prize
Haruspex - Josie/Jocelyn Deane

Local Award
Iphigenia in Triptych - Trisha Pender

Contents

Winner 2021 Newcastle Poetry Prize

Any Saturday, 2021. Running Westward

Lachlan Brown

one-handed pram technique pushing back
the dawn sky's black activewear. feeble pieces
of sleep return or recede like righteous

seismograph measures. the trees arch over
this street as though things could be muted
(the spray of cockatoos shredding leaves/

the gasp of a trailer being dragged toward
the horizon). peripheral decisions create
their own playlists based on the algorithm's

benevolent curation. something should happen
now e.g. double-clicking a window that previously
escaped notice or cursing a phone battery

that drains too quickly after an update. but
instead the sun rises like a petrol light coming on
and the day just autofills. some shopfronts

might change without warning though it's
heaps hard to repaint the high signs. what
is expected when the café installs a rustic

door that leads nowhere? there's a newspaper
for proximate reading with suggested search
terms based on patterns in history:

kayne west wreck it ralph.
kayne west wrestling with God.
kayne west were is he from.

in an adjacent universe runners are tapping out
steady rhythms along the levee while the speaker-
cable of the murrumbidgee winds itself into sky.

it's all about self-optimisation and flightpaths,
the escape route view soundtracked within noise-
cancelling headphones. a platypus quietly drops

back into the water like a forgotten question,
then the galahs descend onto st michael's cathedral
in episodic waves. these shrieks meet open moments

like the bell icon with its red warnings or
the phantom vibration that was nothing, no-
thing at all. responding to grace in this geo-

location becomes a limitless vocation (as task
and counter-task greet the penitent engine).
submit to one another, even when the crossing

lights don't change, even when influencers stop
influencing. the grain of the strava-segmented
world runs towards the three families who own

most of the city (no one can legislate them out
of existence). suspicious eyes begin to appear
everywhere, for instance atop the hospital crane

that seems to traffic darkness to alternate and suit-
able locations. because of the drought it's easier
for a figure to be seen walking over waterways

in the chromatic dreams of the disciples. measuring
stride length could give an approximate value for
speed, height, and distance. sunlight updates sky,

river updates shadows, morning shifts gears with
the calls of magpies as they hop across the path
with adolescent brio (devouring the seeds that

have fallen there). outside car dealerships automatic
sprinklers start spraying turf and concrete at the app-
-ointed time. maybe microgrids offer hope: the climate-

changed dairies harvesting sunlight, the fake wedding
that almost redeems collins park. on some occasions
it's easier to steal than to self-scan, because when

groceries blip in ponderous spondees too much
gets revealed. complaint culture keeps this world
spinning with the learned precision of a rewards pro-

gram. getting to flowerdale on the wiradjuri track
takes a repeat journey. a hidden stile emerges from
the fog like a missed exercise in transposition. carry

on to find fishing rods spearing into the earth, pelicans
swiping confidently on the water's flat surface, the edge
of the frame ghosted by twisted gums. imagine those

prophetic sketches for sale: tone tone semitone
along exposed brick walls slightly shuddering
with every hiss of the steam wand or the precise

gauge of the double-shot grind. progress will arrive
when another landscape fitout meets these industrial
elegies. at least that's what the murmuration of inserted

birds announces, as though the fine print from a cul-
tural plan had been finally set free. tracing the spine
of the golf course and up into pomingalarna the elevation

gains the whole world as kangaroos flick across the track
in search of tagged posts. leaping spirits ricochet from
the ridgeline, morning shafts of light laser through

the scrub illuminating angles that cannot be real. this
crivelli precision annunciates a foraging echidna or
plastic water bottle. each circuit is coloured and graded—

the blue loop, the green loop, the yellow—non-
standard halos with topographical overlays. what
gets seen from such heights? tiny souls escaping

with each expelled breath, or a helicopter arrowing
toward the hospital roof, announcing mukky's *quiet*
uncertain ¬peace? remaining happy and located in a kind

of consumerist way becomes the precision gift of gps,
the single file of spaceX satellites stalking across
the riverina sky making all human achievements

and purchasing options available. those sky-runners
bring kicks to doorsteps, their carbon-miles accreting
in the second and third levels of consciousness.

the horse drinks from a trough without offering
feedback. half-startled when a figure passes close,
the horse takes a step back then statues. crisp air

speaks to horse and runner, reminding both of
the body's fraught edges. it's a screen freeze
moment, the buggy connection looping magpie

calls, the world really present in its pixilation.
tone tone tone semi-tone. scale complete or half-
complete, like a disputed paypal transaction where

the contractor didn't fashion an assessment well
enough to pass. just a lifestyle thing, just another
drug deal at the summit of willans hill, stumbling

into sunrise and station wagons, pretending not
to have noticed anything of significance. of course
official accounts differ: *were is he from?* that temper

trap song rhymes *o riverina* with *everyone can hear ya.*
the surface of lake albert is stretched timpanically thin.
recall the conductor who gripped his baton with both

hands as though swinging a norse weapon? downbeat-
ing the opening of *carmina burana* this way, the *o fortuna*
threatened to tear a hole in the fabric of the universe.

now endless choirs of backyard dogs scamper and growl
when a rock crunches into a corrugated iron fence. sections
of fog ferry rough voices over the waters; when artificial

shorelines are far enough removed everything will dis-
solve into the blessing of algae. do not drink yet (wait
for the moment of redemption). home security feeds

catch a figure cutting through properties, ducking out
of sight. *were is he...?* third member crossing estate bound-
aries, exhaling in time with each land release phrase:

a. buying and looking to build,
b. building and looking to sell,
c. looking and looking and just

looking at the moment. who will be here to carry
the body down to the waters when they are stirred?
community facebook group commenters diagnose

weird visions at dawn or sounds that ominously punctuate
the darkness: uneven footfalls, cracking branches, the skid-
ding of a dirt bike through an empty block. all potential

infiltrations must be monitored, because waiting for
promised infrastructure drags time into unsatisfying
shapes. *allegro con moto* means running the edgelands

of subdivisions, strawberry farms, trails where dumping
is prohibited. the prophecies announce that another
kfc will arise post-covid. the air is already frying itself

in anticipation as bodies sweat and salivate. which
parousia will save? which will lead to damnation?
the apps begin to fund this developmentally beneficial

version of the future. backyard chickens preen
and squawk as though calling their warning to
the slaughtered generations ahead. clipped wings

can't rise over colorbond fences. the fox paws
at the ground in canny desperation. isn't nature great?
on a kitchen bench, a sourdough starter silently exhales,

expanding domestic dreams in instagrammable direct-
ions. b doubles spill grain on the edges of highway do
not glean the edges of your fields. galahs measure the width

of shoulder, the velocity of approaching vehicles,
the artificial winds that whisper them underneath
massive sets of wheels. yet still they eat. and there

are many miles to chew through before waking.
promises, etc. terms and conditions, dull muscle pain,
reminders that something has been achieved that may

not ever arrive. *were is…* think about this rise and fall,
the moment's monument, the line that corrals reality,
and shapes the prayers of setting out and return.

2nd Prize

After 'Still Life with Babette's Jug #2'

Gayelene Carbis

From a painting by Anselm van Rood

You take a white jug and you see shadows, blues and greys hover
like halos, like surfaces, like ghosts at the edge of boundaries,
a thin curving handle like an ear you can see through,
shapes and triangles of roses and cerulean blue and then black,
and then the ear becomes an inverted tear, or a cartoon balloon
for someone to speak, and now the body of the jug's smudges
take on qualities of the moon while the rim fills with aqua blue
to swim in, and yet that centering of white is not where you begin
for it's obvious it's oranges in their bright bold orbs that verge on
the lusciousness of peaches in a brown bowl, and how brown is not
after all boring but the comfort of wood and blocks and warm
and a sprig of green sits in a corner like a talisman, like a surprise
of spring and the light as a touch feather amongst solid things,
and you place three pears on a soft-yellow plate, round blobs
of bright green, and yellow-greens merging into each other, and
then the one that is orange on one side and greenyellow on the
other, as if someone has come and spliced it in half with a colour
wand, it sits there not divided but whole in its two coloured selves,
and they sit together like siblings, like matryoshka dolls, waiting
and the bare suggestion of silver blade and black handle of a knife
lying across the plate like something that might be used but could
be left, and you take a tall orange bottle but this isn't the orange
of oranges, this is deeper and darker, something that suggests and
almost seeps into the splash of red beside it, and then you have two
pink blocks, like books, one on top of the other, or breadboards,
this light lovely pink that's soft and strange, you don't often see
this shade that shines like a light on water in a pink sun, but pale,

but not pallid, but bright, and there you place a golden bottle,
as if you have taken the yellow-orange blaze of the sun and
burnished it, brought it here to warm the soft pinkness of slabs,
shapes that are round and voluptuous on top of squares and
surrounded by rectangles and triangles and edges of things,
there is no beginning here, not oranges, not a bright white jug,
possibly it's a table, you start with what's solid then move to
what you put onto it, this table that is verdant green grass,
something for every orange and yellow and gold and pink to
sit down, as if stable, as if called upon and summoned, but only
perhaps for this moment, and then you notice even the gold
has a tiny triangle, like a tease, a taste of pink, like a flickering
page, a suggestion, as if the solid pinkness of slabs have leapt
out of their boxes, a butterfly's wings leaving its imprint
on gold, and then there are other shapes that suggest tables,
dimensions, depth, this cobalt blue so bright, so shimmering,
and then the bottle with its limbs and its shoulders standing
there, almost the same colour, and yet not, its lines both
blurred and clear and surrounded, right next to olive green,
two bottle-shapes, their bodies lightly touching, and close,
like lovers, and tall and slim, in the background, but sure,
and then more squares and more cobalt blue and tables almost
on top of tables, as in some higher, some lower, and all together,
and the suddenness of two black bowls of small oranges, one
large and high, almost a bucket, a gigantic cup, and the other
smaller, rounder, and only one with a half-sun of lemon,
and inside both bowls that luminous white, that smooth shiny
suggestion again, and on a bright white square sits a green-lemon
something, a perfect circle with softly blurred edges, a serviette
or placemat seems too ordinary to sit on this table and yet everything
that's ordinary and extraordinary is simultaneously suggested, as
you take all these shapes and colours and place them seemingly
randomly alongside and amongst each other, and we don't know
where to begin, except everywhere, and you have given us everything.

3rd Prize

ataraxia

Christopher (Kit) Kelen

1
in a clearing, just of hours
the one patch hoped for, blue

we go round with a see-through moon
you go with me in a fold map mulched through

the place is water, spirit pointed in clouds
everything stands up from that

truth dips and perches
years fallow to it

there's landing in reflections
at times a stillness rounds

2
valley in the lines to spare

first to mud
then with the gloves, down where time is

nudge adjusting, mote in beam
eyes shielded, blade in hand it rings

one round chipping, one just squiz
with clippers then by gumboot

3
from tuck of creek, sun
climbs out of thicket

patched with weft, to loose limbed ramble,
you go with me by accidents, as if

play of scale confounds
a tendril rise calligraphy

tangle of only up

4
look in
flower, vine lift heads

let lines run to a tune
glance sideways for the edgewise

having once brushed, join the dots
or else it's automatically

conjure for presence a thing half tended
like Mercator's firmament

it's all backyard—tilled, wilted with
what's missing, called as such

5
come into summer
then slash and let it range until the haircut

do always easiest first, go once round blank
thought resistant... nothing to see if you don't look

for headlines, how the kettle calls
we who are deaf to doubt come wonder

fallen through autumn leads on to this
make tracks so you'll have been before

6
roofs are for falling, take your time
the way the twig bends to the breeze

all the definite articles—strange signs
as if I were foreshadowed

the place my pudding unexhausted
knock three times it's yours

all touched and hushed—just leave it

7
even and if not myself
no harm in tending one of those things

you get good at by doing
in the barrow's hands always waiting to hold

destiny bright because it stutters, wants the phrase
it's hard to tell ruins from what's on the way

when we're the fauna in the window
in eyes most meaning—let's go there

amid the green, if stood like stars
in deaths of trees for distance

eternity where we are guessed
nor either is that centre

frogs who come from nothing
are singing just to be

8
this is the place by heart
let things themselves add up

with each round slower, day revolves
wonder of nothing just to be still

sit for the country, landscape dissolves
fences soak into the soil

never saw the big sea coming, never knew the wind
real marvels are all sober waking, everyone knows that

9
more of it letting than dwelt upon
meaning in which to persist

one has to believe in what can be done
day by day till it goes unnoticed   so

you won't tell it's time
for everything as it comes   grown in

like blade and fire gone to ground
I live in the land imagined

ceremony just goes on
we're sorry and we're glad we're here

constant in kindred, breath of
world else surplus to our now

10
in shoes and socks
the quiet noting, wise to do

or barefoot, have a mind to the breeze
cloud cone of insects—sparks eddy

a forest of rain by stages fallen
there's this someone who wants to kiss me thing

see olive drab, see mulberry tussling
adversity of tractor swipe

at possum's ladder up to night
where possum is long gone

11
see how rain is held to the tip
brushed with that light

and wet dog shake of it
the pick-up round, twigs sticks for fire

and little logs from happenstance
tempted to burn one's seat

(so mark winter's middle)
notice the coming-through-the-fence

in what's to burn the swamphens pile
instinctively for

things spring where they had to be
so quicken   build from edges in

till the view's all furniture
ducks won't know what pond I am

12
then somewhere in the afternoon
you bump into the sun, excuse me

it's that way golden, pumpkins patched
clock winding down has whispers yet

one must admit it lights a way
in whim a chase around

prank passing into memory
and not our own   so vanish

13
till you ferment
you'll see tail if

trickling top of the hat for a start
heard upstairs like typewriter keys

it's as if one had slipped under the wire
stayed this long while so that a voice took on

I'm so slight it all grows round
some turn to ache and others itch

here I am in flesh

14
one round to tug and then to tend
with hat, for zephyr treetops

arrange the work as to be solved
set about at a certain stage

you're armpits up in
privilege of the day

music concocted air and breath
of all the energy that ever was

that's how we see into beyond
art of everything breaks faith

to bring by the beautiful brink
and with it sink and swim

15
step out to the plan
be in the ever after

there's one more time around for luck
day lifts to mist, grass fades to fern

thud paws—call this the argument
five kinds of bird change tree

in the warmth of long since fires
nothing thing-at-a-time

16
our fault we let the light grow out
I won't remember here

none sweeter than of your own grown tree
a place like this is somewhere

17
and sometimes in it forget who to be
whiff of the way till there

when you can't sleep it's with you
how is there an end at all

when the last moment's yours to inhabit?
(wings, wheels and welcome! Christmases!)

we're the one more truth to tell
it is good to have met in this place

18
morning then, where day's to do
something heavy duty has had snout at by shed

who's not against me's here recalled
let's take them standing in their sap

or when did the unseen arrive?
and how will we be smoke?

dew set in a shaft to catch
chatter piles on like leaves then

bush lemon high, and you reach in
under these diacritics

turn book upside down and see
the moon's touch taken for cloud

this sky's many fronded
get a wash for free

19
proud to have grown a bit of forest
in time that was quite spare

country welcomes where we have been
    and eaten alive

indoors ants think rain   who'll argue?
illusions amount to civilization

20
one way and another
all who were dreamt plead to

just this glimpse the all-we-have
you feel like living forever

where we go out in the garden

Commended

Autumn medications

Greg McLaren

After Du Fu

1
After Spencer P Jones

Codral Day & Night Cold & Flu,
dexamphetamine, panadol, panadeine,
aspirin, disprin, hot toddy, Corona,
whisky (Irish), antiseptic powder, Mersyndol,
Amoxycillin, Azithromycin, street speed,
nicotine, Hollandia, butterscotch schnapps,
Kahlua, caffeine, valerian, melatonin, oxycodone,
oxytocin. Wattle blossoms. There. Thanks. Thanks.

2
The wall in late sun's the colour heroin feels like.
All day, it feels like – follow The Plough to the re-up.
Listen for sirens, drop the burner – gutter it if you can.
That time, eight months clean – hopeless in the end,
smelling of myself, lank against the muralled walls.
That old Chinese guy down the shops – is that a pipa he's playing?
The faux cobblestones catch the creeping moonlight:
it slides up from Rushcutters, tails you everywhere.

3
This suburb begins with W. Of course it does. Dawn
during iso, down the gully again to the river to just sit.
I've swallowed my past, felt it jet through
in my blood – it eddies there, mid-stream, afloat.
My memory's shit, now, mostly, but that's
a guess, isn't it? There are archives, I could check.
But why do I still resent old friends I never see? It's all
melodramatic, back there, a silly tomb. Want to come with?

4

Cabra's got its own rules, I guess, and, like
anywhere, what happens makes other things happen.
Someone always rising, another falls, or's toppled –
who ever buys out at a time of their own choosing?
Rounding up supply across the west – quite a fucken job,
getting lines clear through the back streets and phone booths,
keeping the authorities quietish. Sniffle as the cold
seasons drift in. I sometimes think – what else could I have done?

5

Unassuming place, until, that is, you step
through, and your eyes adjust – *No sunglasses, please.*
She descends the back steps, jade-tinted contacts,
which is weird at first – smoke rings in orbit.
Each room's screened-off from the other – it's a need-
to-know basis. I feel sun-warm, late autumn, and shouldn't
have before coming. The water feature cuts a chill,
up close. Seen her face – now I'm marked. Ship it, move it out.

6

My smacked mouth looks like a tumbling gorge,
teeth all awry and wrong-angled. How many years
of this shit I do to myself. My life's become mist. Ha.
I missed my chance. I thought I was a little lotus but all
those little sorrows piled up. So: cover them up, bit by bit.
Started out on sly pills, nothing much, but oxies
for the back pain, later. Those distant white gulls whirpooled me.
I wish my parents'd never took us to Ballarat.

7
Who knows when the Alamein Fountain went up.
Probably flags, solemnity, empire's other stiff biscuits.
Those idle girls in its splashing moon, stoned
all autumn, the seasons that follow, if they make it,
if they even stay. Low clouds absorb light.
Powdered rouge and cheap coke flashed with who knows –
not my thing, so I'd pass, thanks. Cars pass – us all
moving between them, on a chance, looking to hook.

8
It's a circle game, isn't it, from here to there.
Making your way home again across the mountains,
past the temporary rivers where crops extend
their golden surplus to trucks, freight cars, parrots
and waves of mice: a handful of grain can sustain a city of bugs.
Nights come, skimming across your slower life:
you're a boat touching at the surface of a waterhole,
your whitening head just floats, looking in. It's so near.

Commended

Poem for My Ancestors

Eileen Chong

Write for your people, they tell me.

My people of the river delta.
My people of the crossed seas.

Northern people who became
Southern people—*no people*

*

My people who lost their language.
My people carved out new worlds.

Grandfathers of grandfathers:
illegible words in a ledger.

The order of misspelled names
written wrong on all the forms.

I call these names in the night.
My people, I cry. *My people*—

There is no answer.
They are long cold in the earth.

They are far beyond any communion.

*

There was no funeral like my grandfather's.
Nothing went up in smoke except for her body.

No blankets embroidered with Chinese
characters hung up like before. Even

the crematorium had a facelift—the soft
glow of lamps, the inside cavernous with pews.

At the front, no cross or altar: just space, and the furnace.

*

A family on a boat. Ashes in a bright
red bundle. Prayers, a Buddhist monk,

his rung bell. The hour her ashes were released
into the sea, we were in the ocean, the water

sucking at our feet. We looked across to the horizon.
All bodies of water are connected, I lied. *She is with us now.*

Her hand cold in mine as she cried for her mother.

*

A magpie one day; a currawong the next.
Cockatoos screamed and wheeled away.

Which bird was her spirit made manifest?
No song I heard turned into dream.

The cuckoo in the red clock nodded to the hours.

*

We arrived in the rain, and drove for miles
away from the city. Outside the cemetery gates,

we gathered handfuls of wild daisies. The sun
burned in the thin sky. Headstones like giant

crusted fingertips thrust from beneath the earth.
He stopped: *my grandparents*—I bent to place

the flowers at their graves, and pulled at the weeds.
Nettles stung my hands, and I cried out in pain.

He nodded. *It's Tommy and Senga, saying they see you.*

*

A single mahjong tile: mouth shot through
with a spear; a globe spinning on its axis.

Her kitchen in my kitchen; her hands ghostly
on mine. We feed the ones we love. We scrape

our bowls clean. We scrub them white as bone.

*

What does it mean for a life
when you know you will be no one's ancestor?

Hungry every waking minute. We count
the ribs of prisoners-of-war. Bloodlines

blurred like ink on crumpled, clutched tickets.

*

Someday a girl will read this and think
of survival. Another girl once climbed

a mud wall and escaped into the night,
carrying only two pilfered buns

and a fragment of jade from her mother.
She did not know where she would end up.

She began in darkness so I might become light.

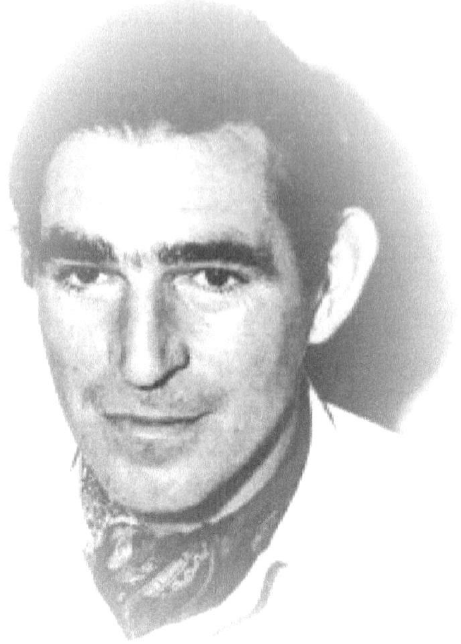

About the Harri Jones Memorial Prize

Thomas Henry (Harri) Jones was born in a remote area of Wales in 1921, the eldest of five children and the only son in a poor rural family. He won scholarships to secondary school in Builth Wells and then to university in Aberystwyth. His studies were interrupted by World War II when he served in the Navy. He met his wife, Madeleine, when they were demobbed after the war. After completing his Master's degree in the post-war years, he taught English to returned servicemen at the Naval Dockyards in Portsmouth, England. He and Madeleine moved to Newcastle NSW in 1959 with their three young daughters. Harri had obtained a lectureship in the Department of English of the then University College of Newcastle, an offshoot of the University of New South Wales. This was meant to be a short-term move, with the hope of returning to Britain when Harri secured a lectureship there.

Harri is a well-known Anglo-Welsh poet and in addition to his books of poetry he is well represented in anthologies of poetry in Australia and elsewhere. He published his first volume of poetry in 1957. His fourth and last was published posthumously in 1966. He was very well regarded as a lecturer despite the alcoholism that marred his latter years and ended with his untimely death by drowning in 1965 at the age of 43. After his death, family and friends donated money in his memory to set up a poetry prize to continue in perpetuity.

Winner, Harri Jones Prize

Haruspex

Josie/Jocelyn Deane

After: Pathologic 2

With six hands, we open the chest
the hinges of rib, the hard monad
of xyphoid, the heavy stone at
the end of history— can you heft it?
will fresh water break out its veins
or roll back to the amphibious root
of the mountain, and we start all
over and over?— to get to your guts.
We are gentle with your cheek, jarring
the small intestine in our hand, we will spin
jejunum, allot ileum perfectly and cut
the end free. We cauterise time. Starlings
undulate like one giant, visible
microbe, each flagellum a tendril we
translate, each bird an eye to absorb
the intertext of juice and bolus, expertly
realised foreshadowing, perfect twists
in the membrane, aminos of theme
and transfat of image entering the blood
stream, chittering in the distance; they
are migrating for winter. Let them carry
the river-bed in their beaks, the patient
lying there, waiting for spoilers, as we
tch over their history/diagnosis, chipping
the rock down with their beak sharp
as carbon compressed to diamond.

Local Award

Iphigenia in Triptych

Trisha Pender

I. Iphigenia in Aulis

in media res

without warning   we are dropped   into the middle of things
in Aulis, the Greek fleet   becalmed for lack of wind   becoming restive
Agamemnon   their leader   flat out of ideas   *we've got to get a wriggle on*

they're on their way to Troy   to rescue Helen
a matter of some import   to Menelaus   his brother, her erstwhile husband

at harbour taverns   the sailors drink   on company coin   and time is money

consulting the oracle

you'd think that they'd know better   than try this route   again
but no   they consult the oracle

the silence of the winds reigns Aulis   we have no power to sail   help us, Seer

to which Calchas replies, seer-like,   sacrifice your daughter, Iphigenia
the weather will be yours   and also Troy

so swift
the ancient bargain
of girl for the world we know
or world we want

follows thence a certain amount of dithering

At first, Agamemnon:
Yes, of course,
let's sacrifice my daughter.
Invite her here to wed Achilles,
accompanied by her mother,
then give her to Diana!
But next:
What was I thinking?
That's my daughter.
My wife will kill me.
And then:
I'll send a letter by this trusty servant saying *changed my mind.*
What could go wrong?

chorus of strange women

if have read or seen *The Hunger Games*   you might recall this classic trope
of girl saves world
the body of the not yet woman   required in sacrifice   to save a troubled state
her blood will oil anew   the creaky machinery   of government
and of course the wind
could be anything
you like to think you need

from our perspective, particularly   troubling
is her zeal for immolation
if we have grown accustomed   to the temerity of fathers
in the matter of daughters   surely, we could expect
some resistance   from the girl herself?
but hark –

turn about

when last we saw him   Agamemnon had repented   his first decision foul   to kill his kin
happily persuading   Menelaus   to turn about
but somehow   in this process   loses faith   has second thoughts
so she's to die once more

Iphigenia rails   with robust rhetoric

Her mother, Clytemnestra   is similarly appalled
and Achilles is brought in   to lend them aid   should manly aid be called for

but second thoughts afflict them too   Iphigenia   considering closely
persuades herself that if her death   will guarantee desired winds
the victory would be hers   and so she wants it

Agamemnon wavering   is bolstered from this unexpected quarter
Dear Father   it would be my pleasure   to save our world in this particular measure
Achilles reconciled by virgin's vaulting valour

II. Iphigenia in England

1556

In irony worthy of the Tudor Reformation
most of Cranmer's most beloved books have washed up here
the Fitzallan schoolroom awash with light and Latin
bestowed on loyal Arundel by new Queen Mary

in the aristocratic pastime of competitive education
it's something of a coup
not even Elizabeth has so much vellum

thus future lords and ladies of the house Jane, Maria, John and John
nested in Nonesuch's golden walls
are with impunity let loose upon the library!

the future Lady Lumley

the future Lady Lumley, Jane will find within this scene
besides her husband the matter for a closet play
and venturing forth from Latin into English into Latin
the rites of adolescence and translation
mutually reaffirming risking nothing

she stumbles on the Greek of Iphigenia
and something like   the ambition of the heroine
encases her   in adamantine

chorus of strange women

That year, the girl whose bloodshed greased the wheels of fortune
was more than metaphor   another Jane   the nine day's queen
succumbed to rampant ambition   on her parents' part
another faulty message system

but under the enabling guise of learning   even girls
can lord it over fathers   offering them up   a mirror for magistrates

Dear Father, as you exceed in dignity all save God,
so I emboldened by my modesty, advise you how the wisest lord in Christendom
is one who learns from daughters dutiful, 'tis better to be read than merely beautiful

To bequeath her play to him as New Year's Gift
might thus have struck Arundel as a boldish move
if he spent time to read it
and with or e'en without   his leave
it set a fashion 'moungst the tricksiest girls
for speaking truth to power
under tribute's guise.

III. Iphigenia in Canberra

you would not believe   the things we've seen   inside this place
bear witness   ye weeping walls   to all their cries
ejaculate   your privilege   in this cup   is that her name?
we'll film it while you do it
the memo said   to clean the couch
it's what we usually do   with stuff like this
I shut the door because   I didn't want people to see her like that
I've thought about it a lot   It's true
I didn't know how to respond   I asked my wife
It's true   I had earlier tried to kill my daughter

There was a lot at stake   I don't expect you to understand

Unbelievable Meme Afterlife

Dan Hogan

With the addition of moon and moonlight,
masked characters and added rain, filth
at midnight makes for a life of prizes. I'm
not a cyborg yet. Homering into the hedge
on six figures, who is the oldest millennial?
Flapping arms around with like-minded
people is proof nostalgia is a political technology.
Accept all cookies? Don't mind if I
do. It's starting to look a lot like ~~Christmas~~
the merger from (つ◔◡◔)つhell ♥ Before
breaking the fourth wall please prove you're
human. Select all squares containing unhappied
transactions. If none, click skip. You only need log
on to squabble mazelike with remembered
information (͡• ͜ʖ ͡•) Select all the shapes
you can while under a frozen lake
and if none tickle your fancy
defrost   Enter all the words below
        with a heartfelt flamethrower. Click verify once
there are
        none. Separate each word with a space. I'm
        not a robot   yet

A testament to the problem of being 'fascinated' (by 'things') at a time of 'cuts'

John Kinsella

For your interest
I (co)incidentally
dropped copies of poems
by Laura Riding & Robert Graves
on the bed for reading
later — that is, I wasn't
overtly thinking

about them as connected,
together, an item,
a partnership
an argument
a passion
a collaboration or agreement
a parsing —

just books off the shelves
as random as possible
because between chores and birds,
between anguish over
dying trees and each little
clearing of each participle
is a filling out with enunciation.

But dropping
the template, I wander
without structure of 'discovery',
random as all get up, or,
the specificity of fine and thickening
roots around an effluent pipe
or one for freshwater alike;

chances are, I won't
see those roots again; chances are
phylums are rewritten
over a few weeks, winter's new
and new sprung rhythms,
the morphing colonial
discursives.

It's how we seem to remember
or forget about pangolins
ferrets, or minks, make
spiritual thesis out of body bits
as suits the sequence,
the agenda: laurels
& gross industrial clouds, labs

of cloth and stone,
(in)vestments
& a way of dealing with / ignoring /
placating / diverting
letters of protest appealing
to conscience — selective (as to which)
trees are lifted out;

I tare and tarry, I tear
ashed edges to assemble
a book of Skelton's, in 'worde
defaced' and 'racid' — to sum
so easily and readily
is throw-away, a scorn
I won't inhabit loving

shapes as crescents and crosses
and overlaps of circles,
as ungiving as giftfoiled
generosity the magpies
unknowing of masks
actually indicates their deep
willingness to get to know you

beyond swoop, broken
glasses, our interspecies
abundance of love,
tolerance, 'sharing' —
each little copse knocked off
forgotten politics shifting
focus as needs be as needs be...?

I don't believe
the claims but feel
the impact of deployments:
excisions and overlays
of wordsounds, racketing
through forms; if you
are capable of hurting

that insect bothering
you, our conversation
will be Pty Ltd,
a vessel for cooking
pesticides by proxy,
and I will hold my breath
till expiry;

it's all there,
coming in and out
of alignment, which
is a gross exaggeration,
the spite of a checker
shadow illusion,
a filing away of reports

of pollutants, decaying
nuclei;
release of matter
without energy
as get up & go
in mornings, 'another day',
each purposeful letter, plosive

of mucosity; love;
loss; building blocks;
and that waking dream
of redistribution — an end
to wealth —; &
post a weaponless
event;

'mystery' as monument
to take cover
behind is the granite
shoved aside to have made
the arena, dislocating
acts of pastoral regression,
the heavy-industry motor roar-scream.

How do you say
yourself in other people's words
or say themselves
for that matter — subtracting
what you disagree with, demi
seeing all, you're left
with broken stanzas,

aren't you? There
are no pens or staples
bolted for melancholia
sources like hayrides
field mice make serious
now, as all nests are,
not flip or style-driven

but who's to say? Merely
pragmatic... what emphasis
lasts the social occasion,
the telling someone
you want to listen
whether they do or don't
and the manners of manners;

by degree, I look
to grain receival points
but they and I don't lessen
hypocrisy via difference
in work habits and joules,
associates, circles,
and sampling tools. Measurements. Quotas.

Disparity
is the spacing between seedlings
in the beds for optimal
chance at growth ('prospering'), as
between reading & writing,
but I only speak
to the limits of voice

under different biospheric
conditions; as if
you took plastic arts
out of ambition you'd
rouse the chorus line
as chanticleer, suddenly
seeing skyscrapers where old

eucalypts break apart after storms,
then the rousing hot winds
that will end me as you read,
as fantails snap mosquitoes
from the page, as pursuit
of weather is a fable
of late grasping for

additional languages,
or augmentations
of whatever you're locked
into. An insect alights
on my forearm but it's a flaying
diode even out here in the country
though it is outdated tech.

So you see what I do
and how and why I do it,
the capeweed's first opening
as blanket statement and its anguishes,
which implicate, and a strand of web
reaching, gently flailing
for an anchorage. I am only outdoors.

Magpies overwhelmed
by earlier insect-rush
won't speculate, and we
share details of presence,
which is neither advocacy
or equity I realise,
though I cede and cede again.

Outdoorery — a door fixation
and *what* a roof actually means
beyond protective coating,
beyond what we read beneath
in bed, under the canopy of collaborative
interaction, pretending not to be
capital; and so we're made

unemployed, we readers. Who
can afford the cutback adjustments?
So, it's out on an ear on a limb,
out among the cerise nimbus of hills —
dragonflies early in weakening eyes —
with recollection and consequence
diffused by chance poems and habitat.

Czernowicz: The Poets

Lesley Lebkowicz

1
Perhaps because I've never been to Cernowicz and will not go,
the city haunts me.
My mother was born there and so,
perhaps because I've never been to Cernowicz and will not go,
when I discover that Ausländer and Celan lived so
close to her—to my mother—and until the war, were free—
and perhaps because I've never been to Cernowicz and will not go,
the city haunts me.

2
All three—my mother and the poets—walked the same streets,
not yet drinking the black milk Ausländer fed Celan.
Of course I wonder, did they meet?
All three—Gisela, Rose and Paul—walked the same streets,
so it's not impossible. For me, it's a hope so sweet,
something to fill the void the murder of my family began.
After all, those three walked the same streets,
not yet drinking the black milk Ausländer fed Celan.

3
I imagine Rose and Gisela arm in arm,
They talk, they laugh. It is a time of peace
and they live in an ancient Jewish city, safe from harm.
It's easy to imagine the two young women arm in arm.
Perhaps, this time, in this place, they'll live at ease
away from heavy boots that smash their pleas.
Imagine Rose and Gisela arm in arm.
They talk, they laugh. It is a time of peace.

Notes:
Rose Ausländer used the phrase 'black milk' in a poem about grief. Paul Celan borowed it for *Todesfuge*. Ausländer, his friend since their time in Cernowicz, was not disconcerted, but generously acknowledged him as the greater poet.

Cernowicz was a centre of Yiddish culture before WWII. It had a large Jewish population: in 1905 sixty percent of the population were Jewish. Rose Ausländer was born there in 1901, Celan in 1920. They became friends.

Dropping in

David Lumsden

1. Blok, St Petersburg

Above his narrow monk-like bed an icon
Hung high in the walls' right-angle, close to the ceiling,
Where in Armageddon or Australia a spider –
No tangler but a hunter – would sit solo,
Likewise by his canal-view desk, so as he worked
Over his shoulder rested the holy gaze of a hollow-
Cheeked abstracted face, editing, rescinding,
An indolent God too peering out windows.

Bergman's bleak lemma crawls to mind – "God is
A spider", an inscrutable *spindel-Gud*
Who lives in landscapes cleansed by apocalypse,
On eucalyptus trunks but is at home on smooth
Vertical plaster walls, and never was
Benign. While sleep brings no soothing void: the poet
Wakes in tears, the reversed telescope of dreams
Confirms flames have deleted his childhood home.

There's no pathway back to the newsreel modern;
There is no track to a grandfather's domain.
Years shut like an amusement park exit, forgotten
And run-down structures; vanished the landowners
And poachers. This brawling in the streets a written
Prophecy does not condone. The burning of poems
Won't help. The Keatsian capabilities
No Caesar gets. New winds fell good trees.

There's Svidrigailov's postulate of eternity,
Like a memory of childhood punishment,
Locked in a cramped old sauna in the garden,
Exiled to its black grimy walls, light absent,
With spiders moving in every corner.
Like wasps roused from their dented wax-ball nest
Or angels in heaven, usages buzz around
And connotations shield each verb and noun.

A night walk in the bush near Lakes Entrance,
Animals' eyes caught bright in the torchbeam:
The foliage shakes as someone adjusts balance,
The twin white stare of one of the protected cherubim:
A sugar glider getting set to pounce
To another tree like an animé hero fullbeam,
And further up yet, the single sapphire glint
Of a hunkering huntsman spider on the trunk.

So let the moon's dead dust shine, Sasha
Alexandrovich would have said, sad and curly
Like Pushkin. Let life bring some small pleasure
Instead to the people, but his soul was all
Bad weather, and his vile blood must be quashed,
He thought. And the ideals crumbled early –
In the combustion of the age, as now
Cyclones hit and fierce winds shred coastal towns.

All that minute lofty detail in the vast
Lost western cathedrals footnotes the upper air
Think of the travail of those medieval gaunt-faced
Professionals, the craftsman contractors
Squinting in dim light, directly supervised
By the Almighty: His myriad jewel eyes glinting
An unending expansionary surveillance,
Constantly pulling uncountable strings.

2. Strindberg, Stockholm

After swarming difficulties, a life
with many bitter changes
is depicted by a well-kept memorial:
a small rotating shelf beside an ordered
writing desk, pens arrayed like soldiers;
the jumble of seven thousand books cleared,
a nest of papers tidied to an archive.

The L.M.Ericsson & Co Stockholms Telefon 5622
no longer brings first night news,
and the summer suit like unprimed canvas
hangs lifeless, idyllic island days
not even memories now, just other people's words.

The white lamp with a red eye
the ill master placed in the window
for the union-organized birthday crowds
stands on an antique table.

Those crowds were soon to tread again
the city's streets for him; this time
without revolutionary anthems,
no roses tossed from the balcony,

but lilies, white,
as on the inscriptionless wreath
he had once sent to the funeral
of the one woman who had stayed.

But that was mysterious history
from a period of poisonous confusion.

His third wife kept away
from the ceremony, preferring to sit
in the park where he had daily walked,
that is, until she left him and then
her new home overlooked it.

Life ends four flights up with a cage lift
and Beethoven's death mask
glaring over the piano, and a large
photo of a favourite daughter
who in the end was raised
in another man's home.

A thing unassuagable, unsoftened.
Nine decades of revaluation rectifies nothing.
Still it is not easy to find the work in English.

Down at the end of Drottninggatan
the waters are always busy.
An installation of blue pipes
invites people to tell their secrets
to the Norrström, Strömmen, Saltsjön ...

Across undark evening, clouds
are massing for tomorrow's rain.

3. Scriabin, Moscow

On Arbát with its pavement artists
offering to sketch faces, their samples
rock singers and Hollywood stars,
young couples are photographed
with Pushkin and Natália Goncharóva.
She looks somewhat wooden
like a ballerina as Coppélia;
he too seems uncomfortable,
not yet a puppet kammerjunker,
but already feeling expenses mount,
uneasy beside his new bride's beauty.

Away from McDonald's and down
a pereúlok is Scriabin's house,
a wall-mounted Ericsson in the corridor.

Watched by an old woman scowling,
visitors can study the biography
summarized in large monolingual placards:
enlarged newspaper clippings
of an early concert career,
old photos, proud teachers' quotes.

In the last room there's a case of books:
one side French, the other Russian,
like the war that had destroyed much of the city.
Another old woman demonstrates
a home-built machine with coloured light-globes,
each pitch with its own colour.
By the exit, audiocassettes
are for sale, labels typed by hand.

The afternoon is failing.
In Novy Arbát cars do forty on the wide sidewalk
and the wild colourful lights of the casinos
blare mad inaudible symphonic poems.

4. Schubert, Vienna

The small last room in his brother's poky place
is open for our curiosity and so we can
confront the question of who gives such gifts
as his, talent being first a weight, a sum,
the Muse's dowry and endowment.
Across the surprisingly narrow street
red flowers sit on the opposite sill.
The place is bare, walls paper white,
floorboards like a grandstave under foot.
Thoughts loiter where the walls
make rounded corners with the ceiling;
the mind elaborates the detail
of how lives play themselves out
between passionate industry and calm:
the pizzicato of the late quintet,
wurst stored between the double windows,
Today in the front room, along
with pages of the Mass in E flat,
the Agnus Dei's quavers like a Pollock
canvas, is the ledger of his coda
months, Franzens Rechnung:
the assets of the pocket
offset against expenditure on sugar,
other groceries, and then
the significantly greater costs
of death and its procedures.

I have become psychologically linked to a humpback whale

Claire Albrecht

I don't know how it happened but I woke one morning tethered
across oceans, over landmass to a very large brain
approximately 4.6 kilograms—not as big as I thought it'd be
but it might have lost something in the transmission

the hook in my own head tugs as I go about my daily things
and the direction slowly moves like an orbit
the whale as he follows his trail north with the shorebirds
is a comet, an explorer before boundaries, while I wash towels

and I don't know enough about string theory to explain how
we might have been pulled together in this manner
or about quantum physics at all, come to think of it
but I know his big whale brain holds 'spindle neurons' just like mine

I imagine these as little blonde girls spinning straw into thoughts
really they are just root systems of neurons that teach us to love
and cry and talk to each other, and it seems beautiful to me
that the whale carries these too, like a songbook

in the night my 1.5kg brain writes poems with him
and we move together beneath the surface of conscious thought
I find myself waking sometimes by the sea, in wet socks
and I wonder if he sleep-swims to the shore like this

by coincidence or design we are the same age
(I can't tell you how I know this, but I do)
the same anxieties swim through our nervous systems
and along the thin silvery cord that connects us

our huge dark eyes stare into the same murky distance
we are afraid of the darkness ahead, but we move always
helped along by the comfort pulled from each other
we're strangers between realms, remote in our seas

I try to talk to him directly, forcing the connection to grow
invite him to daiquiris at the swim-up bar
but I don't know where he is exactly and I don't want him
to end up beached. that is our biggest fear

and it hovers over us daily, a dry eye crusting on sand
stranded, restless, while our body lies paralysed and useless
there is nothing satisfying about rest
we are always rolling the spindle, waving our fins in the air

I don't know why the whale pulls me along
I really don't. all I know is that I am not the frozen head
of an explorer in the Antarctic. not severed, but strung taut
and the instrument of the earth is vibrating

The Dam

Marcelle Freiman

1.

November 1959, holidays on the smallholding where my grandparents lived—
the road in Klipfontein, Boksburg, the house near their general store,
gold-seam lying deep beneath flat country,
horizon of mine dump tailings, fields of straw-coloured grass,
silver poplars along the straight road.

A summer day going swimming, we walked across
the yellow *veld*, towels rolled under our arms, treading sandy paths
through the orchard, the light squinty: flitter of shadows and sunlight,
Highveld noon, the zizz of flies, cricket rasp in the faded grass—
the horse in next-door's field blowing through its nostrils
flapping its lips in the blaze of sun, the crack and scuffle of our sandals
on stony gravel, my brother leading the way.

The dam, a concrete reservoir, fed water to the house, the orchard
loomed ahead like a squat cylinder at the end of the paddock—
soon we were climbing—onto the narrow wall, legs straddling then over,
my feet like little whitish paddles.
In the midday glare tadpoles bumped in rows, their heads a ring of beads
on the wall's edge, a circle of light surrounding the watery darkness:
holding the ladder, I backed in, heels pressed, toes gripping the sludgy coating.

Above our heads the windpump clanked as the wind changed direction,
its tailfin a sail, blades turning lazy and squeaking:
my brother calling out explaining how the pump-shaft
pulled water from the dark ground aquifers.
We hovered, the water tasting of metal and rock,

the boys splashed, ducked under, then up shouting
while I pushed out from the mossy wall, doggie-paddling—
        clouds of itchy-dust came down from the plane trees,
        yellow flecks sprinkling the surface:
with tadpoles and slime of frogspawn we made trails, small circles in the water.

I see us now as if from above, our tiny tracks
sunlit splashes marking an hour in an afternoon, our kicks footprints
        in a timespan, evanescent spray-puffs in the heat of day.
Ducking my face, I could see underwater—the floor thick-layered silt and mud,
        cold through my hair, swimsuit billowing:
        my scurry muddied the sediment, drifting it up,
the water turning murky brown so I could not see—
hurrying back to the concrete wall, the sharp rusty peel of the ladder,
        glad to hear the clank of the wind pump.

Walking home, chatter and peach trees, thrum of bees, a shuddering horse—
        and in early afternoon heat
        the repeated thwack and chop
of Jacob's mattock as he swung then hit against the hard ground
        by the *mielie* patch behind the house -
because this story is also about Jacob,
his English name (I don't remember any other),
        who taught me to greet *dumela* in Sotho,
        helped me see which side of the scale was mine.

2.
Memory fragments: behind fence palings at the garden boundary,
        a low brick building, corrugated iron roof,
chicken-wire pens, a stand of eucalyptus trees:

a row of rooms with a concrete stoop,
built for servants to live in, an enclosure:
a patch of pumpkin vines crawling along the ground, green beans on stakes,
Jacob's wife scooping water with a tin-can from a bucket, the run-off
making runnels
in wheat-coloured dust beneath the plants: the sour-burnt smell
of an outdoor *potje* over coals, black-iron three-legged pot of *mieliepap*—
crumbly grains and tomato gravy on a tin plate, her open hands:
these were days I ate with my fingers,
outside, and was young and questioned nothing.

Jacob was years with my grandparents: lived in those rooms with his family,
worked in the store along the road that led to the clay quarry:
that summer he taught me to fill and clean-fold brown paper packets
then weigh-check using the scales on the store-room bench:
I remember the wrinkling of his eyes, how he'd lean in to my height,
our faces close—I'd match his eye-line with my own,
the brass bowl of the scale, the way we dropped the heavy weights
on the balancing rod, iron wedges and small brass discs thin as pennies,
then tipped in more—*sugar, stamp-mielies,* quarter-pound, half-pound—
the weight of each packet precise.

The memory now a flat bubble in a spirit level measure in time—
when the slow goods-train came by at noon each day
on its way from the quarry to the brickworks—then again at night:
I can still hear the dogs barking
in answer to the faraway echo of the whistle and chuff
as I lay in my bed in the house: night-time, a grid of connections—
my brothers, my grandparents, Jacob, his wife and sons, and the dogs close-by.

3.

Years later, I stepped from my car near a Sydney park—cut loose
from those ties that had meshed my life
in that hard country where things could grow:
ties like torn mosquito netting on a window—my frayed, white memory:
I would not see Jacob's years unfold,
his children ground to their core by apartheid.
This tattered, unfinished fabric I trailed across the Indian Ocean
to this shore: its cords had sunk to the bottom
imperceptible tiny hairline cracks
or mottled patterns marbling a bone: scars that itch and ache each time
I hear the rub of crickets on summer afternoons—

that day at Watsons Bay by a stand of ti-tree bushes and eucalyptus
in a split-second stepping—something opened -
like a crack in the shell of the day—as if in a rush of feathers,
flared past my head—
a tremor in the air shot through from the feldspar and quartz
of the sandstone rocks in this Sydney park
on the rim of the harbour I was held to
by gravity, my heart pumping—
the sudden flash shook me: like a small weight dropping to a scale
it intimated more—that there was more to everything:
the warm afternoon layered infinitely more than itself, a plenitude, stratified
and deep as the shelf of rock I was standing on,
a chance in the weave of that day (any day) to take hold
look again, no matter the grit in my eyes,
for rust-coloured rainwater and a circular dam,
imagine blades turning, cranking a water pump,
cold water beneath the surface of hard country.

Perpetual Cataclysm Machine

Connor Weightman

saved. it is nearly
seven minutes into
Deep Impact (1998) when
the jeep of the astronomer – actor
uncredited – swerves to avoid a truck
and tumbles off the side of the road; he realises
first that the newly discovered comet is on a crash
course with the earth and goes over carrying the sacred
floppy disc. for the course of the narrative his death doesn't
particularly matter, though imdb trivia suggests the scene was a
tribute to comet-hunter eugene shoemaker, whose life ended with
a head-on vehicular collision on the remote tanami track, outback western
australia. hale-bopp was still visible. it was july 1997. at mauna loa 367 parts
of carbon dioxide per million were measured and noted. *that thing is using five hundred*
thousand pounds of fuel remarks an extra watching the rocket propelling the shuttle carrying
the astronauts away from the earth to blow up the comet and rescue humanity. they fail, so traffic
banks to a standstill across multiple lanes of highway. the scene took 2100 volunteers driving
1800 cars and trucks over two days of filming on an unfinished bit of interstate in virginia.
téa leoni as the career-minded news anchor gives up her place on the helicopter to
rendezvous by the ocean with a problematic father. a cg tidal wave smashes

a humble offshore oil rig. the sound techs approximate the demolition
of new york, or they do their best. i reheat curry that's spent
several months in the freezer, a constant energy
supply pumping the heat out. new york
also gets demolished in several
films directed by roland
emmerich, such as
Independence Day (1996),
a hollywoodised *Godzilla* (1998)
and *The Day After Tomorrow* (2004),
the last of which sees the whole earth
— but especially new york — freeze over.
new york is destroyed again in *2012* (2009),
though it plays second fiddle to the obliteration
of california. john cusack's battery won't start. during
those months in the freezer the plastic lid of the container
cracked and i'm wondering if shards of polymer are just now
entering my digestive tract. the ground in los angeles disappears.
the entire anonymous freeway is swallowed by the earth but there's
a love triangle to consider; will the family unit ever be reunited? i treat myself
to the expensive imported icecream sold to us as an ethical-ish comfort indulgence
though owned since 2001 by an enormous multinational conglomerate. they escape
to the himalayas while the visual effects house caresses a destroyer on top of the president.
wade reposts photos from his time in mongolia, says isn't this all a reminder to travel *as much*

as you can, when you can, nothing is ever guaranteed. it's another brutal day of trading
for the brent. in a giant russian plane full of luxury vehicles. *will i see you at the park*
tomorrow? texts liz. the physics seem unconvincing; some finer details are
missing. *do you love him?* asks someone. it's sixteen thousand kilometres
as the crow flies from here to the ice cream factory in vermont.
watch enough of these and you get a strong sense of who
is going to die. only the cruise shipping industry survives.
lauren messages from canberra to say *did you hear?*
bp kwinana is shutting. i send a grimace-faced
emoji. my cousin's husband works there.
600 jobs will be lost, suggests
the article when i find it, buried
behind elections and outbreaks and
several thousand kilometres of continent.
lucy has proposed hanging a giant papier-mâché
model of saturn above wherever we end up celebrating
her birthday. in *Knowing*, also from 2009, measurements of
carbon dioxide oscillating around 386 parts per million, we're to
believe nic cage is a professor. he teaches causality. the film's prophet
doesn't distinguish between accidental, intentional and natural disasters.
next door there's music. icecream, freezer. another unfinished bit of highway
was used for filming a plane crash sequence – this one i've since driven on out near
geelong, some sixty kilometres west of where exxon's altona refinery also recently announced
plans to shut. some of the explosions are real, others painted in post. nic drives to each site of

impending disaster. nic cage's character drives to find answers. i try to juggle tasks while
nic asks the sun: *why did i get this prediction if there's nothing i can do about it?* his car
is five seats and a tray, high above the tarmac. *do you believe in life after love*, asked
cher a decade earlier, if a decade on from playing opposite nic in *Moonstruck*
(1987). suvs initially gained popularity in america for their classification
as "light trucks", exempting manufacturers from the tax applied to
smaller gas-guzzlers. rose byrne is at the petrol station when
an emergency broadcast pulls in every viewer, and then
there's a car collision, two years after starring in
Sunshine (2007), in which the sun similarly
threatens to end all humanity. there was
no pre-existing consumer need for light
trucks at the time, admitted a jeep
director. an attempted getaway
via utility vehicle begins
Dante's Peak, one of two
volcano action-blockbusters to
debut in 1997, the other being simply
titled *Volcano*. 'jevons paradox' describes
how bettering fuel efficiency sometimes leads, in a
roundabout manner, to overall increased consumption.
it's in the passenger seat that pierce brosnan loses his partner
to a headwound, recalling the dramatic murder of james bond's
first wife in *On Her Majesty's Secret Service* (1969) starring george lazenby,

famously forgotten australian bond actor of that single film and shot at a time
when atmospheric carbon was measured at 324 parts per million. lazenby had been
talent-scouted while selling used cars in london. with regards to the volcano, pierce's
character, our hero, wants to apply precaution, but there are business interests to consider.
the volcano might not go off, suggests his boss, though we know the converse to be true, there
being another hour-plus running time. it's only two years later that brosnan's bond is trying to foil
a plot targeting an oil pipeline in *The World is Not Enough* (1999), apparently inspired by the real
bp-led baku to ceyhan pipeline, then in planning stages, through which 700 000 barrels have
moved most days since 2005 across some 1600 kilometres over three countries through
the caucauses from the caspian sea to the mediterranean, a film otherwise notable for
being the seventeenth and final appearance of desmond llewelyn as Q, he who talked
through each gadget and car, dying from a head-on car accident just months beyond
filming. there's time for a frog-in-pot metaphor. time for the earth to make more
of itself. time for love's suggestion conjured by cuts of faces looking
away. barring the occasional shut-down from war, fire, leaks or
other equipment failure. things are shown to be bad when
the cars start crashing into each other. the tiny town's
freeway onramp collapses – again – as i remember
what i was looking for. linda hamilton is good
in this role. the volcanic prop material
was made from bentontite, a clay
used primarily for drilling oil
wells. the petrol station
lights up. a helicopter

explodes. *there isn't*
enough time. this has been
just the longest year. *harry,*
we're on fire. the impressive
sound of cascading water.
lewis hamilton wins the f1
championship again. i haven't
made my bed. they escape via
helicopter into credits. *reunite*
with flight pleads the subject
of the email from the airline. *if you're*
gonna be in melbourne by eleven, you'd
better hurry, sighs anthony perkins' character
ten minutes into *On the Beach* (1959). bitumen
being the preferred oil distillate for binding sand
and gravel in this country. *that's quite a phrase isn't it,*
"these days". berwick is an hour drive south-east of here
through post-1959 infill. sometimes when i'm waiting it feels
boom or bust. economies devoted to one commodity. *can't you see*
it, leaking out of everything? with regards to monogamy i know people
with different opinions. it was fred astaire's first non-dancing role, aged sixty
by the time of the december premier. i've started to suspect i sound a little unhinged.
partially in self-defence it becomes impossible to hold on to knowledge. the experiences
of others. future illnesses. concurrent traumas. *there's a lot of bureaucracy still, you know.*

ava gardner's character looking for love at the end of time. it's when we're apart that i feel
unaccountably, disaster is inevitable. *tell me something,* says liz at odd moments. carbon
dioxide was recorded at just about 318 parts per million, only a year after george keeling
set up regular measurements at the hawaiian volcano. grosjean miraculously avoids
death or major injury in a fiery crash on the first lap in bahrain. still somewhat
higher than pre-industrial levels, though relatively speaking much closer
than where they are now. mum wants to know if i'll fly back for
the holidays. his chassis and fuel tank had been cut through
the middle, leading to a nasty ignition. in san fransisco
they find no cars and no people. he turns off
the power of the refinery before he leaves,
before fred astaire is seen driving a 1955
ferrari monza spider in an end of the
world race, because how else
do you put explosions
in the script before
the implied off-screen
death of everyone. anthony
perkins would later appear with
prolific bond roger moore in *North
Sea Hijack* (1980), eight years before the
piper alpha explosion killed 167. perkins' widow,
berinthia berenson, would later die aboard flight AA11,
flown into the north tower of the world trade center in new

york, 2001. burning jet fuel conveyed by elevator shaft. fred astaire
received an oscar nomination for his role in *The Towering Inferno* (1974), the only
one of his long career, the same year ava gardner appeared in *Earthquake*, where los angeles is
threatened by the titular disaster, a disaster plot echoed at regular intervals in *Volcano* (1997) and
San Andreas (2015). in 2020 an asteroid once more strikes earth in *Greenland*. the readings at
mauna loa inched towards 420 parts per million. everything was said to have stopped. one of
just 35 such cars ever constructed. in *Contagion* (2011) the spread of disease through population
is soundtracked with confident arpeggio. kate winslet performs a search for the words to
describe the problem. the bridge. the airport. cars banked up. aerial shot. *we're just trying
to get in to wisconsin*. my neighbour is looking for his cat, but he did tell me he loves
that movie, even if he can't remember the director's name right at this moment. i see
him again from my window as i'm trying to watch *Armageddon*, the lengthy 1998 asteroid
twin and rival of *Deep Impact*. it begins with a shuttle explosion, twelve years after the challenger
blew on its way up, five before the colombia rapidly disintegrated while re-entering orbit. *anything
can happen in new york.* it is observed. of bruce willis' character, independent oil digger, that
whenever they said it couldn't be drilled, this guy drills it, setting the sound stage
for a series of monologues canvassing an individualism rugged as the ancient
exposed surface of some extra-solar body. i hate this film already,
the thought of finishing pushing me away like all confrontations
with the end do, like all strong messages, accurate and urgent,
about how to change the narrative even as we are in it, do. a
month after texas froze over. another once-in-a-century
flooding event proceeding in queensland. montage on
top of montage. our heroes here getting used to

the equipment. the names of the shuttles are
Freedom and *Independence*. the president's
speech acknowledges some of the wrongs
that make it all possible. a line of cars,
still still still, plainly parked in the
ordinary frame of the window.
the remaining actors reunite
for the briefest celebration
scene, where in the end
the world has been

The Earwig

Audrey Molloy

At Fethard-on-Sea, in the barrack-bare dorm,
I wake to a scuffling sound like a mouse
        in a beauty-board wall.

The sound comes from inside my head.
Alarm flushes in, filling my cisterns with fear—
        that an earwig is piercing the drum of my ear,

thin and translucent as a Japanese paper door,
past machinations, sound forged from air,
        through the labyrinth route to my brain;

that it will chew through, no, *lap up*
the silken-tofu skeins of my temporal lobe,
        leaving an airy and honeycombed bore

the breadth of a pair of leather forewings;
that my faculties will switch off in succession
        like streetlights at dawn:

first, the use of extremities, then my blink reflex—
my corneas hardening like quick-
        drying glue, my senses cauterized,

numb to the rasp of sheets on my knees,
deaf to my roommates' idle breath, my tongue
        a sea slug, dumb to the lateral need

for *help* and *please*, but a scream is flung,
and my eyes, still oddly shiny, spy the legs
        of a girl swinging down from the rim

of her bunk like links of white pudding—
her Patrick Swayze tee-shirt, the thick
        plait falling over her shoulder as she rouses

the others from sleep—and I hear, above internal
burrowing, the pounding of bare feet on tile,
          and my own racing heart as they half-

carry me to the day-bright shower block where the tee-shirted
girl advances in sumo-crouch as though I were rabid,
          brandishing two Kirby grips—loosened

from each of her temples—which she moves like batons
to a silent battle-song, and I know, in some
          (as-yet-unsacked) silo of my mind,

that her utensils will crush the invader
still deeper and, when withdrawn, will be coated
          white and grey; and I hold her at bay—

succeeding through having long arms—and I scream,
this time for *oil, oil*, and the sleep-addled teacher arrives,
          dragged by one hand, and tight in the other

a loden-green bottle, and I watch—as though from the pebble-
dash ceiling—how I'm laid on my side on lavender tiles,
          how they pour the oil in my ear, carefully,

ready to bolt, as though it were water poured into acid,
how the room goes silent, the volume of shrieks
          judged by hands that fly to red-and-navy mouths,

as first the forceps of the insect's rear emerge
and then the creature, in all its plastic-brown entirety,
          is free, momentarily, from the ear, but trapped

in the surface tension of a droplet, prevented
from flight as a pink heel comes down
          and whitish innards smear and float

in greeny-gold like crushed garlic,
the wings like smashed garlic skin; and how we crawl
          back in our bunks and try to sleep,

each with wads of tissue stuffed in our ears,
believing we will never sleep, yet oversleeping,
deaf to the pips of the eight-o'clock news.

*

In years to come, whenever I fail to summon
a person's name or image of a place
I once knew but cannot bring to mind,

I'll think of all the eggs she must have laid,
my tiny one-night stand, the pin-head pearls
she left behind, and how, no matter how

you pound the heel or turn the wings to skin,
you cannot fully kill a thing
that's occupied your mind.

Nefertiti's Missing Left Eye

SJ Finn

The dead millipede got scientists excited
in September.
I watched a simulation of it move,
its woven parts like a wheat spear
or a platted bracelet I'd miss when it
fell from wear.
There was a picture too, the ancient rock grooved
by the creature's commute, indentation true.

That's when I went on a search of everything old
as if it would help me locate myself.
At El-Assasif near Luxor, a cache of coffins
were pulled from the ground, the Book of the Dead
inscribed on the hulls.
The sarcophagi uprooted,
the necropolis brought before the sun.

I read about entombed mummies and looked up
recipes for embalming bodies
You can still buy plant-based confectionary,
Gum Arabic and resin (anti-bacterial)
if you want to make a mix.
I studied examples:
Tjuyu—the famous great-grandmother—
beautifully preserved; a few holes in one ankle,
some scrapes and thinning of her carapace,
but her features—prominent cheekbones
and hooded eyes—distinct.
You can see her overbite as if she died
mid-decision.

There in a touch, a friend sent a link to
her latest art-video.
It's about Lucretius and motes of dust in sunlight.
Her cat appears, its presence unarranged
but broadly predictable if you know how cats
organise their day.
Still, the image which repeats in me is of my friend
sweeping.
The broom is first and then the dustpan taking in
the glob of detritus in one stroke
while the small amount that's left
takes many switches of the brush to gather.
Makes me think of resolve,
but actually it's about time.

I recall Nicaragua,
my partner and I
under a rotating fan watching a film of a woman
shifting dirt on a dirt road with a rake.
You could see where she'd been
but that her work would never be done.
It was the sensation of calm, the balance of repetition,
the idea that time is inconsequential
which isn't to say it doesn't pass
but rather it's not going anywhere.

An old thought rises.
I don't want to be cremated in a kiln.
Rather have my body lying passive in the earth
as if there's momentum in that too
as if the rich ground could be made a little richer.

the lake inside

Jane Skelton

after Beverley Farmer's A Body of Water

The mercury lake
always changing expression,
mirrors all change.

Gold meshes its skin,
trails of moon snails thread the floor—
writing in the mud.

Lapwing family.
No – plague doctors, yellow-masked,
stalking the strandline.

Men fish in silence.
Boats congregate, nose like dogs,
on popular holes.

A cast line, sunlit
spider-thread, tenses – a bite?
No – a sea-grass snag.

The men pump nippers.
Black sand is sucked, disgorged;
the fire's dark strata.

Bleached shells in burnt sand,
spill out of eroded dunes—
blood clams, ancient feasts.

Balawan, mountain,
over the lake, faded blue
torn off shred of sky.
Below the lake's lid
an expanse of green-glade rooms;
velvet touches skin.

Fishes, ghostly shapes,
twist in green, bottle-glass holes;
glimmer, then vanish.

A flathead takes off
as though shot from a pistol—
a smoke-cloud of sand.

A metal torrent.
Sea mullet circle us—
close enough to touch.

A moon snail egg sac,
jelly crescent, bobs on wavelets;
pinpricks glitter – eggs.

Moon in the black lake
sliced into corrugations—
a ladder, skywards.

FORM GUIDE TO THE SOUTH WESTERN SLOPES OF THE GREAT DIVIDE

Kevin Smith

My friend's house, a timber box, stood in a vacant lot. Paint flaked from worn boards. There was no fence, no mailbox. Trail bikes roared across the block, past the house, and up the hills into plantation pine. The wind whispered untold mischief done there. And no witness.

One room is all I recall: a kitchen—in it, a table, a double bunk against a wall. Valerie slept above, her older brother below because of his leg, the polio. I didn't know where my friend slept. At the table his father leaned toward a radio, a rolled-up form guide gripped in his hand. When the horses jumped the starting barrier, he flogged a chair-back with the guide to get a winner home. His stub of pencil smudged out numbers one by one, his fingers stained with nicotine, his tea gone cold.

His cigarette smoke pooled beneath the ceiling like a small storm. He didn't speak. At the stove my friend's mother made up for the shortfall. Valerie had gone out, she said. 'The hell with?' He mashed his smoke into an ashtray and crossed another number off the list. The food was meagre.

My friend left for his granny's house so I went too. We stood her bins on the street, pissed in the gutter and the moon was up.

We chucked stones at her—she in silent vigil over all the things I'd yet to know and what I'd never comprehend. 'What?' said my friend. He stared at me, a stranger. The sky—a black mouth—widened behind him, the stars its broken teeth. Above the town a fire burned on a forested hill, shadows stumbling among the pine.

I slept up top, my friend beneath. I closed my eyes and breathed Valerie in through her pillow and imagined what she might have worn when she left this night, and who she might be kissing now—and if the moon sighed for her—for how a thing could turn from love, now sharp as stones on hard ground, the force of him unkind and blunt. A sudden cold broke and entered. A muffled shriek escaped the night; the world she knew she would not know again.

The house slumped when the lights went out. Beyond a thin curtain, an empty street. Bolted to a power pole, a transformer hummed a long note that rose in darkness as if it might entice the stars to come a little closer. Smoke from mills along the road forsaking town dulled the stars. Inside, the lowest sky I'd yet to sleep beneath.

January

Caroline Williamson

Bossy! Only believe says the weight-loss program
without evidence. Though you do have to listen
if you want results. The body has its own
concerns, spine aching first thing
and a quick weigh-in confirms a problem
continuing. And not getting any younger.
High quality shoes designed in Japan
are like walking on pillows. Why is it good
for the economy to keep on making things
we could live without? Not rationing
but deliberate choice. The Cuba line
on cars, layers of colourful paint
flaking over rust. High-tech meetings:
postage-stamp faces and no air miles.
Nothing stops us except habit. A virus
begins its march through the population
of New South Wales but will they cancel
the fireworks, the crowds at the cricket?
Will they hell. And why would anyone
die in a ditch over a face mask –
blue and white from the pharmacist,
bright cottons hand-assembled. Breath
held steamily to the face. But she is digging
her heels in, digging a hole, can't be seen
to change a mind in public. Freedom yell
the internet angries, feeding off each other,
radiant with self-belief. These are people
who love their children, keep their houses
in good nick, drive cars, are mostly
well liked by their neighbours. Carrying
their stubborn fury like armour. Freedom.

*

You go to bed wondering what will be happening
in the morning, and in the morning you wake up
and over there in another country crowds
have stormed the national seat of government –
predictable, predicted, business of politics
interrupted, lawmakers in gas masks, who knew
they had gas masks under their seats? Some
people think of everything. Is this
a coup, or an outrageous intrusion on what
passes for normal, or a few idiots getting
out of hand for an hour or two – didn't
they have barbed wire round the White House,
where's barbed wire when you need it? I have
myself been involved in the cutting of barbed wire
but that was us not them. How last night
there was a man dressed as a swamp creature
and a placard saying drain the swamp, clever,
and someone with a staffy on a lead. There were
women in red coats and boots in the cold
weather, bit of a party, you could have walked
safely through that crowd. What I am failing
to say. How your body changes in an angry crowd,
your heart rate, your voice, your actions
no longer entirely your own, channelling
the energy of thousands. Us not them.
In these times better to be working at putting
people back together, assessing injuries
in a wounded human, blood pressure, heart rate,
level and location of pain. Identifying
and preventing bleeding by whatever means.
We've been watching reality TV. How a team
of people work together in Emergency: calm,
skilful, each one with a task, using their words.

*

‘I hate saviours I love heroes.’ Alice Notley on
the one who refuses any system, that is the one
who will pick up any useful system, examine
it, use it for a while in a new way then walk
off leaving something unexpected behind –
a new product of that system made extremely well
and abandoned: placed alongside others made in other
ways, as the products of other systems. Orphan
products, no loyalty. The frameworks are there
to be used for what they can do. Don’t come here
for lifelong commitment to anything except
the moment of perception which destabilises
everything else. And bring that into
everyday life: to each human being
that crosses your path, say. Otherwise known
as charm: intense attention, dangling
a little joke in mid-air, unheralded and no
label, no punch line – to see who gets it
and one joke leads to another, or allowing
surprising behaviour to occupy your mind
apropos of nothing. It is as though you left
behind small explosions on very long fuses –
to have been seen clearly and with the same
curiosity you might bring to a work
of literature, say, a poem that will always
escape analysis, resist all intellectual
attempts at definition, continue to be
serenely itself while generations of scholars
apply their best powers of historical analysis,
their explorations of its ambiguities, the other poems
on which it draws, the social conditions that
allowed it to be written. You chose to remain
astonished by the original thing, black type
on a yellowed page slightly tattered at the edges.

*

Oh no too close to the screen and this is IMAX
complete with thundersound, blocking ears
even during the trailers (new Bond, old Marvel).
What is this, Kansas dust storm and real
memories of the real thing in a future drama
so you get those ancient faces, the filmed
interviews in their final years? Or were they
very good actors brought out of retirement?
The last years of the biosphere. Also the last ditch
space exploration, wormhole and a bolted together
interstellar vehicle tankily reminiscent
of the old ute on the farm. Just keeps going
regardless, bits falling off, no visible need
for maintenance. Somehow in moments
of high drama there's always the Stars and Stripes
dead centre in the screen: badge on sleeve
of pilot struggling for control, flag on lonely
outpost on alien planet. She kept the embryos
going throughout, but how will she raise
generations of babies on mankind's new home,
what stories will she read them at night,
what will they have for breakfast? Breathable
air it seems but no sign of vegetation,
no animal life. The perfect colony waiting
for its new masters. Terra nullius. And please,
the father/pilot promised his little daughter
he would come back and he did: on her death bed
at a great age, so that's all right then. Back
through the wormhole to lend a masculine hand
to the nurturer of babies, whose one true love
has conveniently died. Two and a half hours
with fingers close to ears. Well at least I didn't
leave halfway through and upset the rest of the family.

*

You can use it as a way of incorporating
almost anything, and also as a filter for noise,
the perpetual buzzing, the mind picking up
first this and then that complete irrelevance.
Take this week's favourite word: deconvergence
also known as digital detox: pay attention
to the heavy little box of tricks in your hand
and find substitutes for each function. There may
be more on line shopping involved, more
coin batteries. Good quality pencils with
erasers on the end are such a pleasure.
Is there a freestanding digital camera in
the house? The shop where we'd have bought it
has just closed down. When you watch yourself
with that thing in your hand for an hour –
where were you, who else was watching? Opium –
you can write down almost anything
on this page, but if you don't read the deep work
of someone more skilled, read it slowly
and preferably aloud, how will you shift
your mind into working order? It means
discarding as well. And the mind's been busy
recently constructing alternative lives,
while yesterday the Russian at the two-year-old's
birthday told a random group of twenty
and thirty somethings about the Party taking samples
from his typewriter, and how his work could be
ignored, silenced without anything said,
and I was listening, asked him what
do you do then, try samizdat? and none
of the highly educated young had heard the word –
its dripping garlands of Cold War politics, its writers
not much read these days, its impregnable Wall.

The line 'I hate saviours, I love heroes' is from Alice Notley, 'Translation of a Chinese tribute to jade'. *Alice ordered me to be made*, Yellow Press, Chicago 1976, p 47.

Predictions

Gregory Horne

> Memories are not mere records of the past. Biologically speaking, they are about the past but they are for the future. They are, all of them, in their essence, *predictions* aimed at meeting our needs.

Mark Solms, 'The Hidden Spring'

> It's a Tokyo bouncy ball
> It's an Oslo bouncy ball
> It's a Rio de Janiero bouncy ball
> Filter, I love these mighty oaks, don't you?
> Do everything and feel nothing.

Dry Cleaning, 'Scratchcard Lanyard'

When you tell a woman who loves you
some secret ancient shame, she is likely to
reassure you with an embrace.

Likelihoods are not certainties,
in the same way that not all metallic tastes
are the taste of blood.

Olives in a bowl, pleasantries follow.
Expressions of kindness are well received
when motivations are after-thoughts.

A mug will feel as heavy as it did the last time
you lifted it, not heavier. As muscle ages,
everything gets heavier in increments.

Old memories are the worn cards
in our decks, but the older ones, the inherited ones,
are shiny with wear, balustrades & steps we use to pull ourselves higher.

If I engage in text, I will be prompted to think;
& while we can be open to thinking differently
our whole lives, instinct comes before thought -

the eyes of disapproval can flicker or glare,
it doesn't matter that it is an instant; a coin-flare
in a fountain is the sun in your eye.

A touch of element or iron takes place once.
And there are other recollections we'll return to daily;
experience is uneven terrain, so watch your footing.

My memory has recently improved, I'm not sure why;
opened like a richly perfumed flower, a blushing lily.
I keep playing the old songs that I know will make me cry.

Hot winds in the morning lead to hotter afternoons -
some thoughts tend the same way, scorching
like asphalt or dark sand. Leap!

to a shady bole to find your rest. We can't be angry
all the day. You used to take long cloud-gazing
sessions in June, on a warm trampoline.

You bought & built a trampoline to pass that along,
you brought home a dog. You live in a forest
because of how you feel walking through one.

To gratify is the safest thing a person can do.
Even at our most vulnerable, we are either
bottoms or tops. Call it The Relentless Tussle.

If you find yourself in conflict with a friend,
look to the most recent transgression as its source.
Unspeakable utterances sit touching this -

the worn supports that lift us, are also crutches
when we're unsure of footing. Hold on tight!
It is possible to be a transgression.

Art, & any act of creation, is a form of seeking,
& thankfully, of play. I just can't remember
how much of me I'm responsible for, can you?

But I do know the rules. Always been a quick learner,
a quicker forgetter. Song lyrics
are the most irrelevant instances of language,

& dancing is proof of this. 'Man! I Feel Like A Woman!'
by Shania Twain can be a popular song
at weddings. Singing along is unnecessary.

Is it difficult to say exactly what you mean by dancing?
Dancing is a freedom we allow ourselves,
but how we do it, there are rules for that too.

The only teenagers who love jazz music
are those who can play it. Why is that?
How long can a dangerous thought hold its breath?

On a good day, I could go the length & a half
of your average backyard pool. We both liked to dolphin
kick & dive to touch the PebbleCrete.

I think we've proven to ourselves that it's possible
to get where we need to go, without knowing
how to get there. To step outside, is to remember

having done it before. I remember love vividly,
- spraying your perfume is a simple spell -
am I wrong to predict its end, or its return?

The Search for the Darling Pea

Duncan Hose

Your eyelashes ticklish like the frosted collagen
Flaking off the huge horns of an ambling Ram
God
future humid Buzzing prairie grass steppe nations of the Grass Family
Raucous
Haze of Raptorous vision
'Are you my Hairy Darling Pea?

Lieutenant Dougal Beatty, decommissioned from the RMC
<Royal Marines>
Taken a land grant at 'Brighton' and has one assigned
Convict, Molly Pewter of Tipperary, whom he refuses
To buy underwear to soften the chase of her coarse
Work-dress and smock
'I'm sweating down me bumcrack!'   a rare and fine commodity

Who are having a Weld-gun that is smoulder-line
Tin and nickel and lead and salt and condensed-milk-
on-the-moosh affair

It is strictly forbidden to have an affair with one's
Assigned convicts remembers Lt. (Retired) Beatty
As his middle finger breaches her sphincter
To feel himself moving inside her
It's freckles on freckles out there at the Beatty Brighton
Ranch
A Giant Hollywood signe on kunanyi/ Mount Wellington thassays:
B U M R A T T Y

'Should I call you 'Boss?'   'Sir?'
'Yes Leftennant Beatty Sir'   'Yes Commandant'

She were taken away from him and sent first to Arlington
Then to Launceston to serve in a Quaker household
He abducted her*   she whose nubility physical and metaphysical
Made him sticky-eyed
They went to live as Fugitives at the 'Bay of Fires'
Subsisting on Lobster, Abalone, inedible leeks and potato flowers, cockles rude
Rude scallops and shipwreck whiskey

Thir illegally wrought union brought seven children: Pat   Ken   Shirl
Kaye   Shazza   Rod   and   Pinkie Macgillicutty
Everyone got walkie-talkies for Christymas
'Are you my Hairy Darling Pea?'

Howd they spend there days? ask the bored children
Lookingout the High Deco Windows at Glittering Sydney
The children played at infamy
She smoked the punky flowers of the Indian Hemp in a small straight
white pipe & he

drank test-tubes of Cretan grappa heated with Cretan Honey
and composted sea-chanteys 'bout catching uncontested
the left-handers sprawling through the bay upon whose name
Even the Palawa people could not agree

Their long and long Romantic history consists of two outings:
Once down to Barton Estate to partake in a killer-colonial orgy
Once down to Hobart Town* to see Martin Cash

* on a pale horse named 'The Shane McGowan'

With a ropearound his neck
Sing his last full Chantey
& savour   the sweet sting on the lips of fresh nicotine

'Is he enough of a Road Rage Scruff to qualify
As the Beloved?'
'Are you my Hairy Darling Pea?'   the gap in the front
teeth known as 'knacker's gold' &
'the future of paradise'
'La Porte bichette'

CHORUS: VOICES OF SYDNEY SCHOLLERCHILDREN:
Can you do it Dougal Beatty can you change yursself into
Anythink?
You bet the sweat
peculiar pickle tha'buckles
The centre of your Ass I can !!

We Salute you Melody Pewter and your Man
Slung with a tiny apocalyptic harp
Dung-gold Beatty

Dougal Beatty: River Phoenix
Molly Pewter: Martha Plimpton
Pat Ken Shirl Kaye Shazza Rod: themelves
Pinki MacGillicutty: Willowsticks McPhee

Horse Wrangler: Kirsty MacColl
Leisure Supervisor: Redmond Barry
Directeur de la photographie: Wyatt
Mise-en scene: Chick Cobra
Snake Wrangler: Uncle Jack Maynard

Fox wake

Nicole Rain Sellers

Kalaroo fire trail

i

You died at the tiger snake crossing, a coastal brink between
urban and wild, near a broken shopping trolley, front feet bent
on the track, outrunning a truck, your apex predator. Felted
fur makes a dull bed; only your head still the mythic red
of a devilish wetland stud. Dandelion pompoms arc
your lush tail, too proud for its withered body.

A ranger has slashed grass rings around you
rather than push you into the sedge. Defiant
canines frame your black lips, snout soft orange,
chin white-tipped, limned eye sockets half-closed,
ears pricked toward the spirit world. Bittersweet
belly sinews curve over dirt to your haunch,
rich house of larvae and blue soldier flies.

Casuarina catkins blow ochre dust. I am just another invader,
Vulpes vulpes, another vulgar hunter introduced for sport, but

I gather branches to cover you, build you a fine needle bed
on the law of this place, bring you banksia re-entry rights.
Grass torn from your den threshold, dry and green ferns
sweep a way from the wastewater plant to mangroves

where foxes lurk like tigers. A lomandra spike
seeds your return, armloads of brindle sand
ground you, paperbark sheets record your stories,
blackberry stains your history sweet, bitou allows
smooth passage, tea tree ecstasy. Hakea to slip in
between, plantain to heal your fugitive wounds.
I speak to the hush: Let it be known that

this fox was a loved part of this ecosystem, respected
by trees and animals, by rubble tracks that guided
his paws, by swamp that hid and held him in mud.
Frogs sang his infamy, little wattlebirds frenzied
the saltbushes while he pillaged their eggs.

Bring him back to these burrows, shrubs grown in his scats, rabbits lost
and caught, his underworld exits concealed by weeds, to the earth
that fed him, that he feeds in return. Let him rummage in mulch,
dig pungent dens, curl with his siblings in bracken. Let his kits
become rivals, let vixens remember his nip. Let him drink at

these creeks again, linger on land that knew his scent,
his bark. Let his spirit return when it's ready.

I plant three stones: death, life, rebirth. You are buried
in tributes, laid in foliage robes. I turn, but a tuft of you
drifts, lands in my path, waits at my feet, matted
red-and-grey strands. I am answered, entangled.
I take the fur home, sing to it, drop it in compost
to boost seedling pumpkins I'll eat this winter,
dreaming of foxes while copper plumbing
carries your atoms back to the swamp.

ii

these tracks know your prey   black drummers steer me by the ears   past a rusted car
exhaust   lagoon wind that raced in your coat   lifts a red eaglehawk   dangling a
rat grown fat in the marsh you're surrendering to   whipbirds wallop the humidity
gnat froths rise from tannin slurry   bulrush tails redden in sun   morph to cotton
cocoons   sway on your good starch roots   creamy insides unravel   you will feed
your own and others   you will not discriminate   flame dragonflies fox the
saplings

you in the leaves   barely visible   tucked in orange paperbark   whiskers and nostrils persist   jaw scissored sideways   as though on a lamb's throat   the rain has flattened you   knifed you   polished your teeth   axe shoulder blade   scythe thigh bone   shine through hardened hide   skull a puzzle bowl   fishbone ferns link vertebrae chain   to the fluke of your hip   your tail an earth bridge   smooth as a kangaroo's

my stone rests in your core   life   red   for your one wilted tail   swamp mahogany plumes multiplicitous   the black death stone has disappeared   the white   rebirth   rolled to the verge   where banksias flash white undersides   I collect shroud leaves   more threshold grass   flecked disintegration sand   pink poison lantana   liquorice fennel   purple verbena you loathed   toxic like we of the edges   suburban walkers and sewage truck drivers   foxes at home here   under the blustery natives

your colours leach out   tiger-stripe the mangroves   clot the honeysuckle   bruise the bend where we met   eyes frozen amber   we stole into leptospermum bronze cuckoo usurpers   a fox skull stared from a stump   at the water-pipe perch   spiral shell midden   where humans and herons litter nutritious carcasses now a drake on Cold Tea Creek   preens his fox-red breast   I blink   swim in your shadows   dance this wake we made   lope   leap   slink home to forage lunch in the garden

iii
femur
cracked
spine cut
your head gravel
scattered by dogs
splintered snout
stray incisor
half grin
ironic
farmer’s friend
in the mouth
of your den
i return
forked jawbone
clinging to skin
cast away shards
charms
for your kits
fetch red
buds

send you well
on your way
unmasked convict
tail sunk
claws
stroke earth
one
talisman tooth
pricks my thumb
remembers
blood
roots pierce
tunnels
twist
i cannot unsee
this labyrinth
grass opens
fireweed
consumes
tiger lilies
swallow us

It takes a mountain to raise a cheese

Rachael Mead

I How to build the Alps

It all begins with stone.
Heat. Pressure. Formation.
Each layer spreading its fresh sheet
over the one below. Foliation is such
an organic word for orogeny.
This was back before flowers.
When words seemed tiny.
Moss. Fern. Lava.
Only fifty million years until
things grew to picture-book size.
Plateosaurus. Ticinosuchus. Ceresiosaurus
Then the extinction. The one before this. Before now.
Bivalves, gastropods and brachiopods don't fare so well.
Diversion. Deformation. Laurasia and Gondwana part ways.
Waters obey physics and Tethys, the Mother of Oceans is born.
Orogenesis. Compression. The Alps have nowhere to go but up.
It sounds sudden, but all the while, flowers are working
the kinks out of pollination. Dinosaurs grow
feathers and a love of wind. Around
here, when you start tunnelling you
find more than grottos of red limestone
or quarries of black shale. Dig deep enough
and you'll find the scaffold of everything.
The pieces that fit together into something
complicated and profound. Fragments
of colour and shape that you can slowly,
painstakingly, with trial and luck,
piece together into water, into sky,
into grass. Memory and desire.
History and perspective.
Ourselves.

II 13 thoughts on Alpine pasture

1. They are the delicate conduits through which the earth feeds itself to the sky.
2. The pasture speaks a hundred languages, its dictionaries running to seed, a cross-pollination of dialects, all with thousands of words for light, microbe and weather.
3. The summer pasture is a gentle thicket, yet to the grasshopper it is a metropolis of stem and space, creating its own climate.
4. They are deceptive. Beneath their wild skin, they hide ancient bones.
5. The valley is a museum; each pasture an artefact preserving artisanal collaborations of ruminant and human.
6. Nothing exists without threat. The woodland, that patient coloniser, lies in wait, desiring nothing more than to stretch itself across these vast beds of grass shining with a harvest of galaxies.
7. Time is counted by various clocks. Summer days pass to the ticking of grass seeds, cowbells ring out the passage of seasons. The mountains sleep through the aeons, occasionally twitching in their dreams. Nothing changes quicker than light.
8. This may look like a world for romantics but at heart it is the land of the pragmatist.
9. Rancière says that looking is not the same as knowing. In these fields, all I know is that you can never step into the same meadow twice.
10. I want to hear the stories of the soil's dark realms, but I do not speak that tongue.
11. I have heard the high pastures called man-made, but the stones hold up the sky.
12. Cow and human alike all bend to the will of the grass.
13. And all the while, the pastures get on with their steady work of spinning cellulose from sunlight.

III Pasture ecology

after Tracy K. Smith 'The Everlasting Self'

The pasture
weathers the flood of light
shedding pollen in every direction —
a seasonal responsibility:
sprouted, unfurled, flowered, then
eaten, absorbed. Like life
from centuries past or dung
a cow has left across the field.

The flood of light weathers
the shedding pollen: sprouted, unfurled, flowered
a seasonal responsibility
like life, eaten
or dung from centuries past.

The flood of light eaten, then absorbed.
Across the field, a cow has left life
or dung in every direction,
shedding pollen from centuries past.
Then eaten — like life, absorbed.
A seasonal responsibility.
In every direction the flood of light.

The pasture
weathers the flood of light
like life or dung
in every direction. A seasonal
responsibility, like a cow
from centuries past. Pollen,
the flood of light, eaten like dung.
Like life in every direction —
sprouted, unfurled, then eaten.
Shedding the flood of light: a seasonal
responsibility. Then eaten like life
from centuries past or dung.
A seasonal responsibility.

The pasture, eaten.
The flood of light sprouted,
unfurled, flowered, absorbed.
Or dung like life across the field
in every direction. Sprouted,
absorbed, like life or dung.
The pasture from centuries past,
a seasonal responsibility — eaten.

IV The inside of a cow

Inside the belly of a cow is a place
untouched by the clean face of the moon.
We are not so different, she and I. Complex and
contingent, we float between subject and object.
No longer just one, we are arrays of bodies,
landscapes for the species travelling with us.
Vibrant matter, we carry worlds within worlds,
our boundaries porous, the microscopic other
redefining our grammar. Our singular is plural.

It is dark. It's dense and industrious. This rumen
is a metropolis for microbes – bacteria, protozoa
and fungi all cohabiting, a collective enterprise
fermenting the green of the fields, cracking
fibres into short chains. Fatty acids. Proteins.
It takes time and a return ticket. Rumination -
such a perfect word for considering the world.

The honeycomb of the reticulum. The leaves
of the omasum. There's an organic theme to life
down here in the dark. Water is filtered away
and finally, the abomasum - the 'true stomach'
in the mouths of omnivores and creatures not
used to digestion as meditation. Enzymes
and acid. The final stage. What is created?
Energy. Gas. Milk for the calf, or, if the calf
is stolen, for the human. Microbes sustain her,
feed her, that vast raft of inner life the fuel

keeping her metabolism alight. Carbon dioxide.
Methane. Shit. The microbes give, then
they take away. Nothing is free.

Her blood is rich, caseins clinked into chains.
Rushing through ever narrowing vessels,
they squeeze from blood to the lumen,
tributaries gathering flow until milk pools
in the pink lake of the udder. Lumen, the light
within, clean face of her internal moon.
She is the sunlit grass and the dark metropolis,
the individual and the populace. My plural self
is a desert island. She is a whole ambling world.

V How to make Taleggio cheese

1. Put down your load. You've lugged its awkwardness so far, knees and back weathering every step up this mountain trail, pace matched to the herd's chiming amble.
2. Once you've straightened and stretched, tend to your herd. You know their names. Watch their joy at finding themselves on this elevated island of sweetness.
3. Scratch your dog behind the ears. She's done well.
4. If you can find a minute among your tasks between the *baita* and the herd, take it. The summer light is long but can't last forever. Fill yourself with this air. See how the mountains layer themselves against the jagged horizon? This set of distances is yours for the summer.
5. And now - the milking. Everyone knows their place.
6. Take the milk inside and stoke the fire. The night will have teeth.
7. Pour the milk into the cauldron. It's cow-warm, so the only heat you have to maintain is your own.
8. Add the rennet. You knew the calf from whose gut it came and remember the rasp of its tongue seeking salt from your skin. When you were a child, your heart was fresh and soft as Agri Valtorta but the years have cured it. Now it is as hard as Pecorino with a rind that is thick but not yet bitter.
9. Give it some time. Drink coffee.

10. When you can draw your grandfather's Bergamasco blade through the milk and see the cut, slice a grid through the curd. Pick up your brass bowl.
11. Scoop the bowl through the curd, wrists circling in a delicate churn. You can't even remember how old you were when your wrists stopped tiring from this. Keep scooping until the curds float like ghostly pebbles in a golden pond of whey.
12. Fetch the cheese cloth from your saddle bags. Line the buckets. The lengths fit perfectly, aged to sepia as if you've used them to strain tea.
13. With the brass bowl, scoop the curds into the buckets. When they are full, lift the cloth, curds hanging like fat puddings.
14. Let the whey drain with a noise like you make outside after a long night of grappa and tales. Keep it. Nothing is wasted. Pour some into the dog's bowl. When she looks at you with those eyes, ice-blue and mud-brown, add a little curd.
15. Place the curd-fat cloth inside the wooden mold on its thin bed of straws. Four bags, a perfect square. Leave it. More will drain.
16. Eat dinner. Feed the fire. The winds are falling off the mountain. Polenta with donkey sauce sits heavy in your belly.
17. Turn the cheeses over. Gently. Then pour some grappa. Sing. The nights up here are long. Keep the *baita* warm. Turn the cheeses. Again. Again. Then, when you settle down to sleep, let the them settle too. Everything finds its best self under its own weight.
18. When you wake, tend to your cows. This cheese must grow used to waiting.
19. Prepare a brine with water, salt and a splash of vinegar. One by one, float the flat squares in the brine and turn. Let them dry.
20. Everything ages in its own way. But first, let it rest. This shouldn't be rushed. Let the cows lick the salt from your hands.
21. Send the cheese down the mountain. It's ready for the next stage. Maturity. A dry, wrinkled skin. Wish it well. You will meet again.

Sorry

Shastra Deo

I haven't yet scaled the fish for dinner, I was caught
up in picking the lemons to slide under the skin, which one
should probably do when the skin is more skin than scale,
but what can I say? You can never pick too many lemons.
I'm sorry I forgot to record the first ten minutes
of the 5PM quiz show that started while you
were walking the dog, I know you like it, and the dog, I'm
sorry I do not labour over the intricacies of dogs, I find
more to love about horses, though I fear them, too, but
it is better to both fear and love, I think, so thank
goodness I am feeling both for you right now! I'm sorry
I didn't hear you come in, I was distracted by the state
of the kitchen, which admittedly was my doing to begin with
when I cleaned out the cutlery drawer searching
for the juicer, the scaler with the wood handle, I see now
that the can opener would have been rather useful
for the dog food, or the tinned peaches we could have
eaten in syrup and evaporated milk, which I much
prefer to the canned fruit salad with the grapes that are
not quite tough enough on the tooth, I'm sorry, I know
you like how those grapes give way when you press your
tongue to the roof of your mouth, like a
grape, I suppose, under a carriage wheel, or underfoot. But I
have always admired the tension a fresh grape's skin maintains
over its flesh, like the skin of a horse's lower leg: horse
legs having barely any subcutaneous tissue, that proud
flesh and all right! I'm sorry for the horses. Most of all
I am sorry you'll have to wake up beside me when
again I may be talking about horses as you watch
the shadow of our lemon tree sway as it

paints itself on the wall above my head, sorry for
you, not myself, who all in all has come out of this life quite
lucky, I'm sorry to be thinking about horses while you think
about the lemons, if there're enough left for two tall glasses of
lemonade for us to drink in the pink afternoon, but
you should check the fridge, perhaps, and I will maybe have
the good sense to tell you I am sorry
I thought of that first.

The Saddest Things are the Most Beautiful

Jane Frank

1

The hydrangeas at Katherine Mansfield's birthplace were a startling blue but the Begonia House at the Botanic Gardens was full of tourists, the tea room a sauna. Preferring a climb, she took a cable car, thought like rain ricocheting against the tin roof to the foot of the hill. She fled to the waterfront through a red chrome door. That day, the harbour was not an ironing board: the water was agitated and the mist refused to lift. No matter which way she looked, the houses blinked like white meercats from briefly sunny slopes and flags billowed outside *Te Papa* as she waited for news of his diagnosis.

2

Now a cold north wind had stopped his outdoor work too. She knew she had no right to compare him with Vincent, but this was his asylum, of sorts. The work had always been a lightning rod for his illness, his once-wellness in the town of wide pastel streets, where the shop awnings trapped deep mauve shadows. That sweep of taupe river that will live on in paintings but that he wouldnt't see again. The man in the next room cried every night. Another kind, helpless inmate in the cells of thin, bald men.

3

She read aloud each evening — a book about wine and war, two favourites combined. She would lift herself above the carnage, imagine wild irises by French railway lines, one minute moving hypnotically in early sun, the next as violent slashes in long strips, violet petals on sword-shaped leaves. That was the kind of path they followed in those last weeks and days — a frantic use of colour and time — bold outlines, odd angles, close-ups of grapes and flowers — still lives. Still life.

4

Afterwards, she realised the world is not liquid. It is a series of rooms filled by gold which measures heartache. She learned the hollow way a space looks when the person who loved it most is gone. The light-yellow walls of the studio, his sketches still taped to easels. Generations of palettes, landscape photographs in rubber-banded stacks. Brushes with perfect pointed tips upright in an old jar she'd decorated with red and lavender flowers as a child, now faded to grey. Boxes of Winsor & Newton tubes with tightly twisted ends. A few you could no longer get.

5

These were the fish of stories, the fish of kindergarten collage lessons, silver milk bottle top eyes. They grin for the camera, these big, rubbery, red Whitsunday fish. Everyone smiles, her father most of all, his face stretched taut with pleasure, his smile exaggerated like the north where he said everything was magnified: colours deeper, beaches whiter, reef fish sweeter, fishing tales taller. These fish had been magicked from the wrinkle-free scrim of blue behind them in the polaroid, only a few distant islands tattooed to its horizon edges. Air warm and heavy: honey on her cheek.

6

Kaleidoscopic nights in the 'good room' burned into her mind— a cataclysmic curve of kangaroo tail and spiralling snake moving from within the limits of the frame. Bread and cake mixed with the imagined cries of frightened birds in flight. Was it the last time he painted in oils? The stylised fury of smoke re-worked. It choreographed a blurry, happy time: on tv, the moon walk, the first heart transplant. Early winter dark. A new baby crying. The safety of his lap. It was the first of their fires but the one that endured. Also singed into her head but softened like a smudged life drawing, and fading — her, him, the black dog. Standing by the pit watching eucalypt branches burn savagely, transfixed as ash billowed up into a garnet sky.

7

It is always the small hours when she returns to the weatherboard house. The garden has the fevered sweat of mid-summer. A low exhaled rasp of acknowledgement or warning from the old bloodwood. Snails snore in cactus pots oblivious to city views and a cat crouches beneath paw paw trunks with a mouse. That pitiless crunch of bone. Daddy long legs twitch on a fibro wall lit moon pale near the back door. The childhood fear of them floods back and she takes the laundry steps in twos. A transistor is muttering talkback in the kitchen and tea is spooning itself into the cheap silver pot that leaks. The red marbled vase is moving its lips wide in a silent scream and the Bronte sisters' faces swim from the framed print on the dining room wall, Bramwell's smudged form zooming into focus.

8

She is calm until she hears the chink of the sweet jar lid and the piano begin to play, sheet music blown across the floor. The earnest seascapes still brood above against the VJs. Open shelves through to the hall have occasional spaces: wide eyes. There are Java ornaments carved from crocodile wood, *dieffenbachia* shadows stamped onto linen lampshades and the red wine goblets edged gilt. Beneath a jewelled sky beyond the open casements, more damask cats convene on the bricks around dewy zinnia beds, the line of purple hills she knows are there leaving a ruffled space between the suburb's banquet of tiny lights and a sequinned moonlit net. The piece ends with drama, and she can hear their voices, a question hanging in the too-still air — *the saddest things are the most beautiful, don't you agree?*

9

She sees the eroding world in layers through rabbit-burrowed dunes and mist across to the distant mass of mountain where forests swell over crags. Clouds swab the sea and the space for remembering diminishes, the shoreline contracting, crumbling. Breakers copperplate seconds, wipe them clean like faces — his and the others' —submerged in textured glass, breaking the surface or sinking haphazardly. A complete picture not visible. Won't ever be. When she turns back to the paleo-dunes, their long grasses whipped flat, she is a stranger and this known geography strangely altered, yet it is a comfort not to know what she'll find past the next undulation of gold — a low-lying isthmus of nesting birds? A shingle-weighted cove darkened by dolomite? A white-washed grave fenced against the tide? A dead elm's bed?

10

She runs down the hill, watching the land compress, towards the cliff's ragged edge where the peninsula curves like a hip and observes a sea eagle disappearing over the beginnings of waves it won't see break. The final beach is a thin salt-crusted fringe stretching inland, its boggy verge sandwiching eugarie casings and black soil. A slender enigma across to shallow brine and a pearly mosaiced sea floor where riddles spill to her, sheltered there from the wind. She drinks at peace through a chalice made of shell.

11

She came here to recover and now the silver strings encircle her, pull tight beneath the arc of her summer ribs. The tide sounds in slow golden beats, sand a linchpin of memory, the wash the tepid grit of her dreams. Breakers are reassuring salt tongues. Aquamarine crashes hard on calico and clouds blacken. The parts of him being gone that she doesn't understand seep charcoal into the sea. At the horizon, lightning fires forks of emerald and the wild surf has the beauty of lace. She is strapped with it to ti-tree, banksia and the smooth granite headland, to what it feels like she has always known.

Alluvial Mining

Grace Yee

Locked down in our respective municipalities, edges braided black, we are following our hunches like sea weavers. I am hungry, but feeling him bristle, afraid to eat.

It's time I stopped pretending – his flame is not a yang, but rather, an arsenal of apprehensions. From the beginning, an entitlement that walks past children drowning in lakes.

Our heads/hearts (indistinguishable) are entirely handmade, our tails machine-stitched. In the early days I loved the vigor, the foliage, even the mind games we played but later,

Afterwards, I lacked the language to articulate food, everyday artefacts, and the angst that beads on the surface of garments.

Some nights there were dreams in side-fastened necks and long loose sleeves, red silk and slip.

~

In Finsbury Park in the 90s I wore shirts buttoned to the right, played the saxophone badly. Back then I was Lady Wielding An Umbrella.

The assortment of male headwear was always diverse, but the generals in black were not my domain. The men who played me were for the most part comic underlings, collectors of night soil.

One, an ex-Russian ballet dancer, alone and impoverished without family or friends, asked me why I wore so many clothes. In an attempt to diversify his income, he pulled out all the nails in my house.

~

In good light and using my unique skillset, this relationship has the belly of a cane toad and the scales of a carp. Under mutinous scrutiny you could say it portends a semblance of love.

Back when alluvial mining was at its peak, anniversaries were airport flowers, and (my) dermatitis worth five supermarket stops for a 200 gram bar free from all the nasties.

Even then, there were dark hours huddled alone in anxious negotiations with string, copper wire, safety pins. I never learned how to do reiki.

~

Now I am lethal: a bat-eating 5ft 4inch Oriental Sliding Door. What have I slammed? Journeys. Titles. Balloons and Groceries. The quality of western embroidery,

Life. The peony is shambolic in spring – there was quite a scattering of them here this week.

On our calendars there are squares for Health, Happiness and Prosperity, for Love and Commitment, Gardens. I cut and paste them all.

~

Scrolling old sweetness, water for silver, to place in a casket behind the museum.

Such is life in a small town

Beth Spencer

They say Joseph Furphy had Shakespeare and the Bible.
I had *Little Women* and my mother's 1930s Sunday School
Prizes. And Miss Pastel at school who read *The Adventures
of the Little Wooden Horse* a chapter a day in the hot little
weatherboard grade two building that sat apart
from the rest of the school, and she and the Little Wooden
Horse filled my shy heart with love to busting.

Later that tiny building had a plaque saying Joseph Furphy
went to school there. Although back then we didn't know
such a famous author had sat in my seat, and wouldn't have
known who he was anyway. Or, if we did, it would have been
because of the water carts. The Little Wooden Horse might have
drawn a Furphy water cart if he'd lived in Australia! However
it turns out Joseph Furphy didn't go to our school after all.

(Just a sad furphy). He was born nearby, though, and went
to school at Kangaroo Ground. We had kangaroos in our top
paddocks too, but our town was named after the river.
Well, not the actual name of this river but the word for river
(eternally flowing water). It turns out that when the man
from the Port Phillip Association pointed at the water
he misunderstood what the Custodians were saying.

So he wrote it down, *Yarra*, and thought this captured it
for all time. Which it did, for them, in a way. But it didn't,
in another way. The Wurundjeri call it *Birr-arrung*. But I didn't
know that then. Someone said William Barak, 'King of the Yarra'
was born in our Glen. (Glen means 'narrow valley', but it
isn't really that narrow). And it turns out Barak was born
at Brushy Creek, which is not so near, although it is

in 'The Valley' (quite a big valley). Barak was named Berek
when he was born, but someone wrote it down wrong, then
added William, and turned Barak into his surname.
And he was *Ngurungaeta*, head man. (No kings. Or lords,
or knights.) But even though he wasn't born here,
you know, I think he might have come to the Glen,
to sit and watch the eternally flowing water, and the wattle

that hung down from the banks and skimmed the surface.
(Wasn't there a man called Joseph Banks? Perhaps he'd like
to sit here too.) Barak was a good story teller, and knew
people all around about. I wonder if William Barak
and Joseph Furphy (and the Little Wooden Horse) ever met.
Maybe they had lunch in the tiny school room
with a teacher just like Miss Pastel cutting up

sandwiches for them. (Miss Pastel who filled my heart.)
With the Little Wooden Horse tethered to the bubble taps
outside, stamping his little wooden feet, eager to get on
with the next chapter (and make back that money he had
worked so hard for down the mines and lost when he had to
flee that bad man and one of his hooves fell off
and all the money trickled out as he ran). Life is hard.

Every Friday we took a bus and went swimming in a pool
fed by Badgers Creek that used to be part of Coranderrk,
which Barak fought so hard to keep for his people when
their lands and waters were stolen. (Did we know that then?)
Then that land was taken from them, too, for a long time,
till they got it back. And the swimming pool was freezing
at 9am because of the creek, which should have been called

Wombat Creek, or Platypus Creek (no badgers). Mostly
though in our town we swam in the river, but nervously,
because we were told that eleven people had drowned
there since the town began. They had sheep wire
strung across it so you could stay on the upstream side
if you didn't want to get swept under the bridge
and down past Melbourne (*Naarm*) and out to sea.

But even on the safe side of the wire there were deep holes
and roots of trees, and it was under and in these that people
got stuck and drowned. There was a family who brought soap.
The bubbles would swirl and linger, before they floated away
and everyone kept a bit away from that family on the
sandy bank. (Is this what 'white washing' means?) I wonder
if Joseph Furphy and Barak swam in that same river as me.

(Can you swim in the same river?) When I am an old lady
I would like to swim in that river. I would like to see
if I can swim to the bank on the other side without getting
tangled in old forgotten wire, or in one of those deep
holes full of eddies. (There was a boy at school called Eddy.
No relation to anyone, as far as I can tell.) The headmaster's
wife at our school said she taught Charles Blackman to paint.

(A famous painter, but not a Blak man). She taught us to paint
too, by squashing our fingers in hers. Every year at the Show
all our paintings looked alike. (No-one asked why.) And now I'm
thinking, where did our farm come from? (Best not to ask.) Our
headmaster told us that he was the one who taught Ron Barassi
to kick a football in Violet Town, which is up the highway and
down the road from Glenrowan, where Ned Kelly was caught.

'Such is Life' said Ned just before they hung him in old
Melbourne Gaol. ('Gaol', such a funny word. A funny goal.)
Although, apparently he didn't say that, after all. The reporters
were too far away to hear what he did say, and someone closer
repeated what they thought he'd said, or should have said,
and the rest just wrote it down. Not too sure about
the Ron Barassi story, either, to tell you the truth.

The Drunk Lady On The Bus Has Just Fallen On Her Face

Gemma Parker

which confirms that she is drunk,
which needed confirming,
being both elegant and well-dressed,
boasting a blinding statement necklace
over an ensemble of cashmere, and silk.
It's hard to believe – *on her face* –

but how else to describe this fall,
from her seat – she was fully seated –
thrown to the floor of the bus
like a bag of potatoes,
tumbling like a loose-limbed toddler?
I suspected it the minute I saw her. *That lady,*

I thought, *that lady is tanked,* and I used tanked
instead of drunk because drunk implies being a drunk
and I know she is, I know it in my bones,
it's so early to be this flush
with a dangerous amount of spirits,
but I don't want to be that unkind… Not yet…

"You right their driver?" She calls,
in a craggy voice,
"You alright there?"
Swaggering up with a sway,
swinging herself back down
into the seat she fell from.

Shake out the tablecloth of her
and a million crumbs fly into the air:
the curious and forthright look
that made her kids feel seen;
the steely way she kept herself busy;
her laugh, never false;

the way she didn't believe in rules;
didn't like other adults.
Didn't even pretend to like them –
the ones who were whole,
and loving,
and secure.

When you lose someone to alcohol,
you actually *lose* them,
and the struggle to locate the misplaced self
can make you so angry.
'Cos maybe you really liked
that brave and hurt person,

the one who wore old cardigans,
cried a lot, and was a bit fat.
And now she's been wiped –
reformatted – surgically enhanced –
brimming with the buzz
of white wine.

It's like the old zombie trope:
loving the moving flesh
of someone long dead.
If you had to smash their skull with an axe,
you wouldn't. You'd pause – horrified –
and be done for.

That's what loving an alcoholic is like.

A horrified, frozen pause.

But doesn't even drunk believe,
deep down somewhere,
that they are a poem? Cresting
the thermals of reality.
The way the world collapses
in on them, the divine centre,

despite the bucking ground,
the eerie silences. Drunk, truly
and regularly drunk,
drunk like it's a religion –
it's like choosing
to be your own muse.

Maybe that is why she glares at me so aggressively,
the drunk lady on the bus,
when I ask if she is okay.
The fall already forgotten.
Me, rupturing her perceived reality
of gilded and effortless flight.

Why would she NOT be okay?
It is furious, that look,
like she wants to scratch my eyes out.
I gaze back
weary, so weary
in the face of that blank fury,

that storm
with only atmospheric pressure

behind it. “It was a big fall,”
I offer, in case she thinks my comment
is sarcastic and loaded.
She just keeps staring at me

so I give up, like I’ve done before,
because what the hell
other choice
do I have? She is
some other kid’s
problem.

And maybe she will be alright soon.
She’ll get a little fat and wear cardigans,
quit smoking, she’ll call on your birthday
and teach your daughter to knit.
She’ll sneak grapes to your son
in the high-chair of the supermarket trolley.

She will no longer catch buses
looking like a TV anchor
loaded up on hard liquor
and energy drinks
bristling with pre-sunrise purpose,
covered in industrial make-up

to cover everything,
tumbling on her face
being weird and mean
to strangers. Then you too
can have this moment:
getting off the bus,

walking away,
wondering vaguely
about the mystery of her,
not even looking
to see where the bus
is headed.

Roadtrip

Natalia Figueroa Barroso

Rainbow Lorikeet and windscreen collide.

Green and red feathers fly,
drifting off into el cielo.
Disembodied meat; plumage and blood.
Blinding carnage.

Papá pushes the emergency lights.

The highway zooms past us.
        "Bloody pájaro!" he yells.
His ink black hair sails in the wind.
His gaze so salty it stings.

Fractured roadmaps upon windshield glass.

Sangre trinkles into shards
cracked like veins.
Sunshine bleeds through
stained red shadows.

Beak, wings, eyes, breast, talons.

Plastic bag reserved for
carsickness, for rubbish.
Now becomes our feathered
accident's resting place.

Cigarette lighter pops right out.

The Winnie Blue blazes from radiant orange to ash black.
Smoke doughnuts puff out Papá's lips
as he flicks his ciggie.
        "The milicos rolled one cigarro onto my cell floor, but no lighter."

Dust clings to the dashboard.

With my right index I draw a road.
A sooty fingerprint marks my fingertip.
I don't know why he tells me these things.
Maybe trauma has an end of sentence date.

All's clean, Papá buckles in.

The sea blue sky, out my window,
is profundo. In its depths
clouds plunge and wash over azul
like the brisa envelops a bird's pinion.

Saline aromas in the air.

Murmurs of waves caressing sand,
surf over my ears.
Burnt wood fires up my
gut, it rumbles.

"Are we there yet Papá?"

Radio frequencies are disrupted,
words cut into static tongue.
A change of gear,
soon we'll be near.

Back window frames new scenery.

The land is parched,
flaked beige soil
like my dry lips.
Into the horizon the sun dips.

McDonald's drive-thru steer into awkwardness.

Greasy fingers, sugar rush, brain freeze.
Bolus stuck to the roof of my mouth.
Monosyllable replies lead to a dead end.
Detour helps conversations descend.

"Pronto we'll get to swim."

The words are choked by his moving tongue
and rotating jaw.
As if speaking with a mouthful
of guilt.

Speakers vibrate over the unanswered.

Mist races up into the charcoal night,
covering us in a blurred clutch.
Fog lights unable to cut through
the dense atmosphere.

Forked road, left or right?

Gregory's under moonlight,
narrow his direction.
Tunnelling his vision.
Alarms throb at Papá's temples.

U-turn back into the familiar.

Or so it seemed.
Until we end up marking dirt
with rubber.
Mucked wipers smear our sight.

Tyre stuck in the mud.

His hardened hands begin to shovel.
Scooping up earth.
Searching for firm ground.
Instead ends up with soiled fists.

Windows are shielded by frost.

My breath dances with starlight,
like a haunting spirit.
Papá takes off his jumper
and wraps his warmth around me.

Disengage ratchet pull up handbrake.

        "Mija, we'll call it a night.
        No cucos outside to dread.
        Papá's here to hold you tight.
        Pretende que is your comfy bed."

Pitstop turns into our destination.

Morning dew frozen onto my
raised body hairs.
I pull the hoodie's cords down,
and cocoon myself in.

Day moon kissed by sunrays.

Seagulls tango over the horizon.
        "In el glovebox there's conflé."
Inside sit miniature packets of Nutri-Grain.
But there's no milk, we eat puffy bricks dry.

All aquatic invertebrates are protected.

No live bait.
Size and bag limits apply.
The ashtray is filled with butts.
        "Al agua pato" — to the water duck.

Crest and trough become one.

The tide is low,
two waves collide.
Orchestrating white foam,
to curl and roar.

I dip my head under.

Salt stings my eyes,
bubbles float towards the sky.
A baitless hook cuts through the water.
Bright yellow fishing line leads me to Papá.

Caught fish convulses towards death.

Its fin slaps at the breeze.
It reminds me of a kite talking in the wind.
A flag at half-mast.
Or white sheets surrendering.

www.ingramcontent.com/pod-product-compliance
Lightning Source LLC
Chambersburg PA
CBHW020326010526
44107CB00054B/1994
9780648850465